Dream Catcher 46

Stairwell Books //

Dream Catcher 46

SUBSCRIPTIONS TO
DREAM CATCHER
MAGAZINE

£15.00 UK (Two issues inc. p&p)
£22.00 Europe
£25.00 USA and Canada

Cheques should be made
payable to **Dream Catcher**
and sent to:

Dream Catcher Subscriptions
161 Lowther Street
York, YO31 7LZ
UK

+44 1904 733767

argillott@gmail.com

www.dreamcatchermagazine.co.uk
@literaryartsmag
www.stairwellbooks.co.uk
@stairwellbooks

Dream Catcher Magazine

Dream Catcher No. 46

ISSN: 1466-9455

Published by Stairwell Books //

ISBN: 978-1-913432-63-8
p11

York UNESCO
City of Media Arts

Contents – Authors

FEATURED ARTIST
ARTIST STATEMENT: DAVID FINNIGAN

Dream Catcher issue 45 was shot through with the hyper realistic art of Imogen Hawgood, this issue has the precisionism of David Finnigan. 'Isms' in painting are a double-edged sword. In this case, they can provide the foothold in, say, a dinner party conversation, that can lead the speaker and addressee to further elucidation and illumination. This can be a beautiful thing, or, to paraphrase Keats, "'Beauty is Truth, Truth Beauty." – that is all / Ye know on earth, and all ye need to know'. Thanks Keats! Allow the 'isms' to get lazy, however, and you're muddying the water, overegging the pudding, or, worst of all, deliberately excluding baffled listeners to further augment your own much more evolved, pedantic poise. This is not a good look.

An overview of the paintings of David Finnigan, however, demands a little grandiloquence, because the paintings are so provocatively good and, like much contemporary poetry, problematic to pigeonhole.

The common ground between the art of Imogen Hawgood and David Finnigan is an intrepidity with what contemporary painting can do, and I find that the proximity of both collections in successive issues not only augment the collections respectively, but highlight the strengths of each other.

David Finnigan's 'Synthesis', the collection featured herein, is characteristically exact, though he is at pains to highlight how his art has evolved…

"These four works represent, for me, a change in the direction of my working practice. While they retain some of the exactitude and realism of my previous work, there is more of a painterly feel to these new pieces. Also, a new aesthetic which exhibits an expressive freedom within the confines of realist painting.

They embrace some of the techniques I have learned and developed in my other non visual creative outlets, particularly from the world of sound."

So it is not just a looser approach to the confines of realist painting, but an amalgamation and superimposition of separate geometric compositions over the existing realist composition. These geometric abstractions, function aesthetically in their own right and they have a force and a dynamic which adds energy.

Visually in isolation these geometric compositions echo the work of the constructivists, the supremacists or even futurism and vorticism from the early twentieth century.

Added together with the realist composition, they 'modulate' the existing work, change the dynamic through the use of the already mentioned energy but equally importantly through the use of colour which is a very powerful tool. The now superimposed compositions 'modulate' each other.

"With regard to the concept of 'modulation' I see a simple parallel in the world of sound with the technique of 'FM' or 'Frequency Modulation' synthesis, which as a side note powered the soundscape of 1980s pop and rock music.

Simply put in 'FM' synthesis one waveform modulates the other wave to create something new. This is what I am attempting visually.

Another important parallel is the idea of 'glitch' a sub-genre of electronic music, which became popular in the 1990s but actually its origins can be traced back all the way to again – futurism, specifically with Luigi Russolo's piece 'The art of noises' (1913).

Here again the concept of 'glitch' I attempt to apply visually to these compositions, in which, as in music where the beat and order of the music is broken and reprocessed so some feeling of order remains, I would like to break up the surface of the two superimposed compositions to break up the order and reprocess it to create something new which has a different rhythm."

Greg McGee

PAGES OF ARTWORK

At the risk of sounding like a Radio 4 'Thought for the Day' speaker, Christmas can be a bitter-sweet time. It's billed by advertisers as Happy Families on speed; and, visiting from Planet Realism, you could be forgiven for thinking it was all matching family pjs, obscenely over-stuffed turkeys, snow that falls softly past twinkling lights (but never melts into slush or freezes into black ice); the seasonal films offer heart-warming epiphanies about finding love in unexpected places, as if the whole of December was some sort of romantic or philanthropic Kinder Surprise. The truth can be colder, darker, even just duller: for those individuals whose family scenarios are dysfunctional, absent, or diminished through death or distance, it can be not the most wonderful time of the year, but the most challenging. Even well-adjusted and contented singletons can be presented as unwanted aliens.

2022 has brought us the mad hubris and economically catastrophic fallout of the 50 day British prime minister; the monstrosities of Putin; climate catastrophe; a new pandemic of infection predominantly affecting school children; poverty, cold, inflation, be-leagured public sector workers forced after more than a decade of austerity to impoverish themselves further by withdrawing their labour; grief 'tap-tap-tapping/on your window' and (as I write) temperatures which obviate the need to plug in the freezer you can't afford to power up. What better way to warm the cockles of your pining heart, and your chilblained toes, than Dream Catcher 46?

With absent friends in mind, I'm dedicating this issue of Dream Catcher to Simon Currie and his family. We were pleased to publish Patrick Lodge's review of Simon's recent collection *Enchanter's Nightshade* in DC 45, a collection described by Patrick as 'well worth a read, not least for Currie's concern for things overlooked and his ability to render them never unimportant.' We had already accepted the poem which opens this issue of Dream Catcher before we heard of Simon's rather unexpected death in the autumn. We send our condolences and best wishes to his family. I'm not sure if editors of literary journals are generally categorized as among 'things overlooked', but Simon's submissions always made you feel you had an important role in his life. The poems he submitted for my consideration were accompanied by long, chatty letters, which showed a lively mind, a sense of humour, a slight sense of astonishment that he was really writing this stuff called poetry, and a warmth towards and interest in other people. These engaging qualities are shown in this issue's posthumously published tribute to a talented and versatile man we were pleased to call 'one of us'.

Throw another pile of un-opened bills on the fire; top up your hot water-bottle; grab a cat or two to bulk out the blanket over your knees, and luxuriate in the season's creative offerings. Indulge in some arm-chair travel (whether on the Victoria tube line, or overseas); find solace in the language of flowers (maybe even be inspired to set up a society for the preservation of weeds, among other persecuted majorities); find the hidden depths in an artist's model. Are you after the respectability of matching chairs, or fired up by memories of love? Do you believe corpses are the most reliable witnesses, or are you holding out for the perfect toast topping? Whether you are wanting to end it all or hoping for a new beginning, I hope you find something to interest, amuse, horrify, or inspire you. And remember, by the time you get this copy, the shortest day will be behind us (unless you are in the Antipodes). 'If winter comes, can spring be far behind.'

Keep sending us your offerings, and our hardworking editorial team will read, re-read, swap, circulate, annotate, and evaluate them in the coming months, with DC 47 expected in its usual mid-summer position.

Hannah Stone

GIMMER CRAG, GREAT LANGDALE, 1955

I've not met Guy before;
at sixteen, a year younger than me,
he has cycled here all the way
from Kendal to take me up.

Roped to him, I face
hard volcanic rock, dove-grey,
paler where exposed.
The ledge traversed in turn,

a crack beckons upwards.
Guy looks down and grins.
Friendly but cautious;
he will save me from falling.

Alone, he'd be up in a trice.
Today, he's got baggage.
The sky is clear, though I see
nothing of Mickleden way below.

The far end of the valley
resembles the stern of a great ship:
an empty wreck. For now my gaze
is fixed on rock, Guy's boots.

At the top we will move on
to crag-sites on Pike of Stickle,
where his family have found
the most unpolished Neolithic axes.

Simon Currie (d. 2022)

seven days stranded
                the aircraft our ocean liner
Jesus in the desert
                trading paperbacks down the aisle
overhead luggage
                coffins for the dead
we waged a war against business class
                ate the rich to survive
sharing rations off plastic trays
                we were down to peanuts
sipping water from plastic cups
                (Styrofoam still makes me shiver)
now we talk to shrinks
                and on late-night chat shows
the Survivors of Flight 101
                they greeted us off the terminal as heroes
stooped and stinking
                waved our names on banners
as we crawled into cars and hospitals
                baths and wheelchairs
we wore our seatbelts fastened
                braced for emergency landing
we were dying
                we all dream of flying

Eve Chancellor

BACK FROM
AMERICA

After the grit and grandeur
of New York and Philadelphia
compelling force-fields
edged by emptiness, by frightening drift
away from the gorgeous skyscrapers
a loud buzz of colour and voices
in magnetic Washington Square
jazz and chess and ramshackle stalls
selling t-shirts and jewellery
as exuberant students dash
past men and women
at the furthest edges of sanity
and beyond –
down and outs more extravagantly down and out
than Europe's homeless;
sad disturbance lingers
between our orgies of art and food
(a dizzying feast of paintings
and especially delicious
my first morning's breakfast:
pumpkin ricotta pancakes
with apple and pear compote
bacon and maple syrup)
fuelling hours of walking
in bright, then humid heat –
ten days of exploration, until

returning after a sixhour night flight
channelled through airport and Underground
my tube thundering to Chalk Farm
I decide to emerge halfway,
in central London.
It's 7 am
a sweet, fresh morning
sunshine and leaves shining
near Leicester Square.
People on bicycles
tranquility and birdsong
just a few cars passing
on the compact streets.
A sudden, surprising,
blissful sensation of beauty
and being at home.

Susan Sciama

7

SEARCH FEE

Seeing me admiring a carousel of postcards
Celebrating Costa Rica's colourful wildlife
A small boy tugged at my shorts ...
Come, mister, I show you!

He led me over the road into a shabby
Park where dusty tufts of grass
Poked through the dry bald earth
Like hair from the ears of the old men

There who, punch drunk under the thumping
Sun, dozed on banquettes of crumbling
Concrete and cracked shiny tile.
My sudden guide pointed to the top

Of a very tall tree where, slightly more
Dynamic than its postcard apotheosis,
A sloth performed its morning T'ai Chi
Routine with the patience of a glacier

And the sangfroid of one disdainful
Of the capuchins' heated agitation.
¡Aye, qué lindo! I offered, in top-notch
Yorkshire Spanish, cartwheeling briefly

To articulate the inverted exclamation
Mark (I'm a hopeless monoglot but
An athletic one), *one dollar*, he shot
Back, deadpan, in flawless American.

Howard Jeeves

You say a weed's a harmless plant that chance
has placed where we'd prefer it not to grow;

that time and tides, fair winds and lucky stars
guide fishing fleets dispersed by storms, to home.

Your country is an island, so you speak
in images of sailing and the sea;

your people love their gardens: every weekend –
when they've time – they dig and sow and weed.

We have no shores: our meagre land's enclosed
by other lands. We till it to survive;

weeds steal the water, space and sun we need.
And so we bear down hard and root out those

who'd do us harm. We don't wait for the tide;
and keep a sharpened blade at hand, for weeds.

Phil Vernon

When the shining caballeros
came and smote
their unknowing enemies
with forged steel,
the split skulls and hacked limbs
were offerings
to a new distempered
and voracious god.

When the trappers staked
the woods and dandled
glittering baubles
over ancestral soil,
the multiplying pelts
and quietening forests
signalled new precincts
for a temple in the making.

When the burgeoning towns
along the coast spread
filaments of road
through levelled hinterlands,
distortion and depletion
became rituals,
a softening up
for a new dispensation.

And as the faith expanded,
putting to sword and bullet
the obdurate non-believers,
a vaster space was made
of the rolling grassland,
cleared of its large creatures,
for a nave-like core
of epic length and breadth.

Finally, an altar of buried gold,
facing west, not east,
with chancels either side
of forest and green valley:
a monument to the new creed's
bold, incontinent spread,
a testament to the Word's
fleshly expropriation.

Lawrence Mathias

The New World – Lawrence Mathias

DO WE FIGHT
(Wallingford 1646)

for a city king,
blurred head on coin,
or for our harvests in
and no more burning crops?

My broad hands, trained
for casting millet seeds
and scything in the yield,
now clasp a musket.

This hefty gun
has ritual steps
like liturgy in church:
lead ball, black powder,

prime, ram, present.
But even when my musket
gets to fire its sulphurous load,
the shot sails high,

– more grief to pigeons
than to parliamentary men,
most of whom I know.
Thomas the brewer,

a man of thin beer,
Robert from beyond the copse
and William the fellmonger
whose word I trust.

Not all gunshots miss:
our screams are real.
Those leaders fight with words,
our bodies break and yield.

Note: A Fellmonger is a dealer in sheepskins

Richard Lister

CAMOUFLAGE

In combat jacket and trousers a homeless man's
on the edge of a small crowd watching a band perform
in Winchester High Street, conspicuous.
Three discarded doughnuts in a row on the ground
like a minimalist artwork. The man
picks one up, offering the piece
he tears off to his dog. In the moment it says no,
the man looks at me, sitting ten yards away
with my wife, embarrassed for him; lonely, I think.
But as the crowd starts dancing, he disappears,
somehow blending in to all that colour and movement.
I wonder whose conscience will be pricked next
when he steps out again onto a blank canvass,
white as our innocence, dressed for battle.

Geoffrey Loe

A DEMONSTRATION OF HYSTERIA
(after a painting by Andre Brouillet of Professor Charcot, neurologist at the Salpetriere hospital, and pioneer of psychology and neurology)

There he is, demonstrating theories of hysteria,
his subject Marie Witman – 'Blanche' he calls her
to protect her anonymity, though unsuccessfully.
He is front line, flinging wide the gates of mind,
his audience all male, times being what they are,
a studious crowd – suppressed erotic charge.

'Blanche' is swooning, bosom half-revealed,
propped up by acolyte and nurse. His protégé
is guaranteed to give the goods – he calls her
'Empress of Hysteria', 'Napoleon of Neurosis',
dismisses notions of the malady as 'women's ills'.
This demonstration by hypnosis is highly fashionable,
if rather dubious, to modern eyes, but he, true pioneer,
is prising back the claws of mind's distress.

Poor 'Blanche', product of a wretched childhood,
hungry, sick, abused – no wonder she is in asylum
(where she at least finds shelter, bed and food).
Here is Charcot's ideal subject, he trains her like a pet –
if she acts wilful he will lock her up –
she quickly learns what is required,
an adept at a swift hypnosis.

Blanche becomes a blazing star,
le tout Paris enthralled. She knows the sounds to make,
say of a dog, a bird, kisses a statue of a man,
lets her clothes slip off. But automaton?
No, she keeps control; if he annoys her
she turns the tables back. Gossips claim collusion,
fraud, but this is never proved. After his death
her symptoms cease, she turns to life and work:
becomes a radiographer at Salpetriere where,
in time, the radiation kills her.

Robin Ford

DON'T LET THE NUDE
(After Lawrence Ferlinghetti)

catch a cold, Auguste!
    cried his wife.

But Renoir was hard of hearing
                        and famous.

The older he got
            the deafer he was
                        and the more famous he became.

But the nude didn't complain
                        displayed

her plumpness and her curves

Auguste's favored subject

            so
stirred up

the old man kept on painting
                        the naked lady

        ignoring his wife's call.

The picture was still wet
    when he lay with her

as painters do with their models

and
            needless to say
                        the nude caught a cold.

Don't YOU catch her cold!
                              yelled Madame Renoir.

Too late
  he took to his bed
                        never left it.

What Madame Renoir didn't anticipate:

                                    her husband's death would
make the nude

immortal.

Marie Papier

THE PEARL
(After
Vermeer's
painting
c1665)

Looking back at us
across the void of time
half turned
against bone black
her inner radiance glows.

Her eyes meet ours. They shine
with youth and innocence.
Her head swathed
in the fabric of a former age
astonishes
with presence here and now.

Whether portrait or type
– the Dutch *tronie* – in antique dress;
whether she wears a priceless gem
or polished tin as some suggest,

paint turned to flesh
in this conceit so vivid,
so divine
that we are hushed
to catch the breath that seems to come
from her half open lips.

Several centuries have vanished
since the alchemy was sparked by light
falling on her face and ornament.

Labour of hand and brush and sight,
an artist's skill, defined
her skin, her features, the lustrous jewel
that points her worth
reflecting all her world,

ground pigments;
ochres, ultramarine, charcoal, lead white
a camera more expressive
and more real
than any selfie image
of a girl.

Andria Jane Cooke

MORPHS OF
THE MIND
*(after
Tanktotem vi/
David
Smith/1957/,
Museo
Nacional
Centro de
Arte Reina,
Sofia)*

The *weight on my mind.*
It was a metaphor.
Exact measurements didn't apply.
Images were private theatre.

But then arrived The Day of Manifestation.
When the sun rose, we could look, examine,
point above each other's heads,
compare burdens, witness the forms of our concerns.

Everyone could see Donald carried only a flat cap.
A sweet blue cupcake rested on Martha's head.
Bearing only stems of straw and moon daisies,
no wonder the Johnsons sang like freed birds.

But Virginia carried a tower of thick plates,
so tall we could hardly believe it didn't fall.
How did she even start to steer
around the supermarket of her life?

Lisa wobbled under a slashed tyre.
Ian sat squat under his grandfather's lifelong anvil.
Siobhan tottered at the base of a flag-less flagpole.
Liam's crown was a sculpture of barbed wire.

Whole families had hair cluttered with broken machinery,
like the long grass of upland crofts.
Some fragments were barely identifiable.
"What's that you're worried about?" we asked.

"I'm not sure," Henry answered. "It's been there so long,
like great-uncle's pre-war thistle reaper
left at the field edge on rocky ground,
rusting into abstraction, lingering history".

"Can't you simply reach up and remove it?" we asked.
And then we suddenly thought, "Can't everyone do that?"
And, in a moment of glorious elation,
everyone reached up, stretched and tried.

Only to find the shapes were no longer visible,
gone like accidentally deleted paragraphs.
But nobody was helped: the morphs
had only reverted to metaphor.

Seth Crook

Critical Mass

Mr Blake, I thank Miss Pickford for our introduction.
A bold lady, she stepped into the breach to play host.
She did have some concerns, of course.
Miss Pickford was no artist, domestic science
was her forte, and your forthright esotericism
seemed a daunting change of gear.

Such doubt was unwarranted, of course,
our entry to your world was most adroit.
Practical Miss Pickford ushered us gracefully through
companies of angels on the flaming Surrey hills.
We passed prophets and druids arrayed in white robes,
gaunt and elegant guardians of Eden's portal.
Inside, we found Adam naming the beasts,
and later anguished Cain tearing at his scalp.

It's taken time to reach you, Mr Blake,
and certainly not on that occasion. Our kindly guide
took us into your visionary garden only.
We stood before its epic pathways, the murmur
of a heavenly host among flowers of paradise,
and I knew I'd revisit frequently,
a bright-eyed inductee, eager to explore.

So, I've fashioned my own bow of burnished gold,
and kept a frugal quiver stock of arrows.
An ocean of business to cross, as ever,
in between my visits, the water deeper and broader
than your day, but I always made the journey.
And finally we met, Mr Blake, pure serendipity in the end,
and not where I expected: a consort of angels
sang from the gallery as I sketched in the nave of St James,
and you looked on indulgently, just over my shoulder.

Lawrence Mathias

Sketching with Mr Blake in St James, Piccadilly – Lawrence Mathias

WRITER

Then all those things he never said
to her, to anyone, but wrote them down

because his pen found words
more surely than his tongue

because he hated to compete
to make ways into conversation

wouldn't accept not being heard
or having people talk across him

because he needed time
to find just what it was he wished to say

because he couldn't trust how speech
came out, how words might sound

and, if he wrote it down, there was no need
for looking anybody in the eye.

Tony Lucas

The bassoons fart at the suggestion,
But it's hard to spell –
Phphphooophph tailing off, but deeper,
The sneer ruder, and prolonged – phbrophraccuphbrhbrh.
In this, beauty is ever and over undermined,
As if we no longer deserve it.

The bassoons are sneering at me.
War drums still call the shots –
What's left of the tune is resistance.
At last it dawns, as dreams do and must,
That it is not a symphony at all,
But the world making sounds.

Peter Datyner

We lived to the beat of
our own hearts, under clouds
of gold, we sun kissed ones.
Baby boomers, breath of
innocence, post war optimism,
like kids in an Ealing comedy.
Close to nature knowing every ditch,
wild flower and which tree to climb.
In Spring we picked primroses, violets,
cowslips, bunches of nature's joy.
Frogspawn floated on every pond
like tapioca pudding.
Spit on dock leaves soothed nettle stings,
sweet nectar was sucked from pink
clover and white nettle flowers.

We blew dandelion clocks,
wildly inaccurate but
no one had a real wrist watch.
The white milk in dandelion stems
will stain you forever!
I just had to, didn't I?
On the way home from school
I knelt and pulled up a stem,
rubbed the tip on my thigh
just above the knee – my frock hem
easily hid the mark.
It has stayed with me always
ever since I was nine.
Not an age spot, just –
A dandelion kiss.

Heather Murphy

The layered grandeur of this city
surrounded our pissed-up student life
improvised, cosy, entangled –
transformed our small preoccupations
into sweeping vistas.
Small?
Rousseau, Camus,
echoes of Foucault
fermented excitement.
We longed to change society
our lives could be as grand, as intricate,
as our new beloved city –
walking tipsy 3am
up the Royal Mile
to Gordon's Trattoria.

Yet on a recent visit, forty years later,
I notice this:

A baby rat hops
quite unafraid
by the heaped rubbish
below bright billboards
framing the kiosk
on the central path to the Meadows.

The rats I have seen
slink, furtively dash
from a human step –
this one, innocent, young
is enjoying the sunlight,
rich crumbs from the kiosk
curiosity quivering
in its tail and whiskers.

Susan Sciama

He closed the door of the packing shed and stood
in darkness – waiting for the dense silence
to smother echoes of music and banter.

He lit a candle – walked along narrow aisles, feeling
warm air swirling like incense as he stooped and gently
pulled rhubarb stems from their crowns, like giving a blessing.

He often paused, as if in deference to the silence,
to listen for the muffled pop - pop - pop as buds
gave birth to emerging shoots.

He shuffled back along the aisles, snuffed out the candle,
opened the door, his arms full of bright pink, juicy spears
tipped with golden flames.

Alwyn Gornall

Carmel surveys her garden. She shrinks into the security of her back door porch as she watches it growing at tropical, not temperate, speed.

It's like fast-forwarding a horror film on television. Her eyes narrow as she focuses on the hairy coils of ferns unfolding like serpents, their dotted sporangia swelling. She's spent years waging war against the ferns. Grating her spade against the rock beneath peaty soil. Balancing on its handle like a child on a seesaw, to try and lever the tough black roots from their iron-fist grasp on her flower beds.

The terrible groaning of the resisting rhizome and the sickening crunch of pearly pink-brown snail shells beneath her feet, still play on repeat in her mind. Recently she'd taken to beheading the fronds with secateurs, but the ferns continued their conquest, and she hated the caustic stickiness of the sap on her fingers, its stinging dark-green smell.

Her azalea's crimson flowers are crisped brown, they flap despondently like crumpled wastepaper caught in the shrub's branches.

The lawn, which used to be neat and trim, cut as regularly as her own hair, is unkempt. The lawnmower, an old friend, has become a heavy foe who bruises her legs and makes her arms ache.

Encamped in a clearing Carmel's hydrangea sprawls, circled by tall grasses, their sage plumes bobbing as if on the helmets of an invading cavalry. Emerald leaves, fashioned with a neat trim and tailored point, try unsuccessfully to maintain order amid riotous blue pompom blooms.

Even the intense soprano perfume and silky beauty of the pink roses do not cheer Carmel. Their stems twist like barbed wire, thorns clawing cruelly at the soft summer air.

"Your garden is looking lovely. Lush." Hortense's voice thuds like a cricket ball hitting earth and Carmel ducks, but she can't dodge her neighbour's face which is clearly visible above the hedge.

"It's buzzing with insects, humming with life. Real wildlife garden."

Glossy buttercups catch Carmel's eye, waving to her on slender stems. Beneath their bright yellow petals, violets polka-dot the grass. Purple foxgloves with white speckled linings sway amongst a host of self-seeded orange poppies. She imagines a figure in an impressionist painting, surrounded by swathes of colour.

Carmel thanks Hortense for the compliment and slips quickly into her kitchen. The pot of tea she brews is very satisfying, sweet and refreshing.

The next day her visiting son frowns as he looks at Carmel's Garden.

"Don't you like gardening anymore? Is it getting too much for you, Mum?"

Carmel smiles and she talks about biodiversity. Her son has an artificial lawn.

She does not tell him about the spiky brown ball she saw nestled amongst leaves when looking out of her bedroom window at dusk. Or that she dreamed of hedgehogs and woke up happy.

Alison Milner

It's more like telepathy. When I deadhead an Albertine rose,
mum whispers in my ear from another garden. When I bend down
to smell the Mock Orange, my brother, (I swear he laughs up there
in the blue beyond), brags about his Morning Glory, how it blazed
in his back yard. When I rub my fingers along a Mint or Lavender
leaf all the little bees in my life sing like Van the Nan and happiness
is a Red Admiral, a proboscis sucking nectar from a Buddleia. When
I trowel in the dirt to find life from last year's Beyond Blue Salvia, or
my Apple of Peru, and there's no sign of life, I wonder what went wrong,
if I upset our friendship? I know I've done such things before, opened
my mouth wide, let the world know what I love or hate.

Today I've planted a cutting, a white Love-in-a-Mist to remember
you all by, friends who walked out the garden for good. When I move
my pots of yellow Cosmos or maroon Penstemon to a shadier spot
under the Copper Beech, take in a deep breath of acceptance, you
wouldn't believe the serenity of talking to flowers.

Penny Sharman

Fox

Where fox fire flamed
shedding the last minutes
of the December sun

drops of light fly
from the dark pine trees;
rain drops on the wind

of a moon-washed night.
Then after the long
cold hours of darkness

a hint of grey haunts
the horizon, and a fox
sits at the very edge of dawn

waiting   watching

Bridget Thomasin

Fleeing Scandinavia's snow and ice
they come, riding a strong north-easterly –
little specks flying over the crest-crazed sea
on course set by their own inner compasses
for the east coast of England.

In the slap and flap of wind,
as the sea ruptures onto the beach,
they reach land, buff bodies lifting
and falling, flashing patches
of black white yellow. Waxwings

drop exhausted in village gardens
to jab and gobble berries from cotoneasters,
pyracanthas. Then they're off.
I follow, twisting my head this way
and that in the blustery wind, scarf unfurling,

in an impromptu dance back
to the marsh path, where the wind eases
to a fizmer in the reed beds:
a flash of yellow again, edging black tails,
and sealing-wax red as they land on sea buckthorn.

One sits alone, self-possessed;
its crest blown on end, punk-style;
its deep-set eyes bespectacled
with black lines
have the stern look of a Victorian cleric.

With its feet clamped to a branch,
feathers puffed-out, apricot blush on buff,
it sways, rocked by the wind.

Christine Selwyn

Just one of those starlings, peace bring me the words,
that flock around the church's tower, bleed
airwards into murmurations and with one voice
return upon its pinnacles, just one of them,
while wind whips static trees to shapes
and sun glints from feather to gold grave-grass,
would tell me what I want to know
and could not bear to hear: how life is miracle
and miracle is everything upon the eye,
grass knows, too much sometimes.
We have shortened our resistance in wires
and fed till drunk on cow's first cream,
too much, stone knows, to bear sometimes
the murmuration with one million-voice.
Just one of those starlings circling round those stones
has all the answers that I ever asked.
The graveyard grass is golden, listening.

Simon Beech

So now you've your legs in the air
In the grasses of a damp back yard –
Not much dignity there, old table
And the rain has glamoured them like spray-on tan

High days had you polished as a debutante
The odd washable spill was unavoidable
The tickle of the fingertip tripping on your grain
The caressing cloth wiping you down

You're folding into the fuck-you earth
From my window you're a spectacle
Those well-turned shins and ankles starting to streak
You're like a sad ballad sung to a drunk

Not what you were, no, when the playing-cards
Breathed heavy in the wee hours
Before the cigarette-burns, infuriating age spots
And an infant sadist knifed in his initials for good measure

I suppose that sadist was me –
You were ill-used, when I come to think of it
Taken for granted, part of the furniture; now
Crudely up-ended, left standing on your head.

Fred Johnston

APPLIED MATHEMATICS

I. Success

For every 100 kilometres we advance
across this 100 kilometre front
we gain 10,000 kilometres squared
we must supply, control, administer, defend
from outside and from in;

look back towards.

We're simply winning,
until we start to lose.

II. Under siege

The roads are closed
and foraging for water, food and fuel's unsafe.
But there's a way.

Each day we'll halve
the rations that remain,
use half, and store what's left.

Then in the morning,
start again.

III. Probability

There must be traitors in a war.
If you don't know their names
arrest the ones from where
betrayal would, most likely, occur:
women and men whose mothers and fathers
we likely arrested before.

IV. Rectilinear

On straight and narrow roads
through forest,
marsh or mud

the target zone's
as wide as
the convoy's long

and when the road is blocked,
the convoy's speed
is none.

V. Threes

A rifle,
a magazine, three spares,
in the hands of a soldier knowing only what they're for

are worth
the same times three
in the hands of a soldier knowing why he's there;

and in defence,
compared with attack,
worth three times more.

So what's the worth –
compared with silence, drumbeat and
the calculus of harm –

of a voice,
a call for peace
and the courage of those who stand apart?

*Note for Stanza V : À la guerre les trois quarts sont des affaires morales ;
la balance des forces réelles n'est que pour un autre quart.* Napoléon
Bonaparte, 1808.

Phil Vernon

TUBE SPREE

Hot even for June
and the door of my fridge fell off
not without warning

and nothing for it
but Tottenham Hale Retail Park
a very long way on the Tube,

not crowded and just as well
for three old men
very drunk

who cast aside their shoes and socks
as Pimlico flew by,

who sweated cobs at Warren Street
where almost every stitch came off
three fat bodies
pink and clean as the day.

Hot even for June
and boxers sufficed
for three old men
riding the Tube

from Brixton to Walthamstow Central
and back

from Brixton —

Jenny Hockey

Eatin' yon book wi' yer nose, like,
he'd have said, with his crook smile,
the back of his hand broadly veined and willing.

So we did, deeply, the both of us – one
siphoning up the illusion of horse
and space and a whole not-likely country;
the other snuffing up sci-fi in sly bursts, the drug
that could book-beat raw bruises, life.

Still do. Still does
the job: soon as you open them, inhale
the else of them. The anywhere but.

Angela Arnold

Low Pitch

I recommend shoes as great flower pots.
giving umph to the prosaic terrace –
a family growing together once more.

Sons and daughters in far-flung jobs
left behind these leather selves, these imperatives,
each an intimate tiptoe memory store.

Granddad's wellington, on the very dot
of Spring, will thrum with Allium, Narcissus
and the Lenten rose, or Hellebore.

Gran's court shoe, glitzed by a sequin caught
on her wedding day, looks June in the face
with Pincushion flowers on show.

I can turn my son toward the sun, glad I've got
this bespoke link, a criss-cross lace
of memories – poppies in August.

Daughter's pointe shoes, worn even in her cot,
beguile in mid-September. A Slipper orchid sways
above pink wings. Worth waiting for.

I glance at my own Greek sandals. Wonder what
they'll nurture when I'm gone. Will they embrace
Galium verum – lady's bedstraw?

Philip Burton

Dreams have flown – migrating birds.
Nothing here matches. The carpet and curtains
Have holes or else stains.
Even her children don't share a last name.

Her sons are in trouble, more often than not
– Regulars both at the pub and in court.
Fighting each other, when no-one else there.
Brotherly love! But still loyal – to her!

She keeps things together, maintains the façade;
Setting the table. It's just a charade.
Nobody eats in the other ones' presence;
Up to their rooms like anonymous tenants.

What does she pray for – to make all seem right?
Conflicts' cessation; end poverty's plight?
Love; empowerment; peace in the world?
No! – Flowers in the vase, and matching chairs.

DM Street

"Excuse me, but would you mind sitting somewhere else?"
Tony looked around the waiting room to see who had spoken – but could see no-one. He was not surprised that he could see no-one. There had been no-one in the room when he had arrived just a few moments ago. Having selected a magazine to distract him while he waited, he had the choice of half a dozen chairs of various shapes and sizes. Indeed, there was a greater variety of chairs than there was of magazines: half a dozen each of *Homes & Gardens*, *Ideal Homes*, *Woman & Home*, a dog-eared *Country Life* and a couple of *Cosmopolitan*s. He had finally settled on a *Cosmopolitan* (there might be a questionnaire in it, and they were always good for a laugh) and had settled comfortably into a high-backed, buttoned, leather chair with padded armrests.

Shaking his head in puzzlement, he flicked through until he found *'What is your sex IQ?'* and perused the opening blurb.

"I'm sorry to be a nuisance. Normally I wouldn't ask – but it's been a stressful day and you look an accommodating fellow." The voice was doleful and world-weary.

Tony looked around again. No-one. He leaned back so that he could see underneath the chairs opposite. No-one. Feigning an air of casual interest, he leaned forward towards the coffee table on which the magazines had been scattered, checking that there was no-one hiding underneath his own seat or the seats to either side. There was not.

"Hello?" he queried, as he reached inside his jacket for his phone. Perhaps he had inadvertently called someone by mistake. But no. Pressing the button that activated the device, he was greeted by a rather ordinary home-screen. He really should get around to personalising it sometime.

With another shake of his head, Tony turned his attention to question one. *'Is it possible for a guy to have multiple orgasms?'*

"Oh well. I suppose if you're comfortable …" The voice sounded woeful, "It's just my back, you see … After a hard day … Still, never mind …"

"Who is this?" Tony asked, closing the magazine but keeping his finger in the page. (He wasn't sure about the answer and wanted to check it out later.) "And where are you, for goodness sake?"

"Right here, of course. You're sitting on me."

Involuntarily, Tony leapt to his feet, spinning around to look – at the empty chair.

"Oh, that is so much better," the voice was somewhat less mournful, "You have no idea."

Tony edged around the coffee table, keeping a suspicious eye on the chair he had just vacated.

"This is a wind-up, right?" he laughed nervously, "Like that whatsisname on Sunday night telly. You know, the camp one that skips around the stage. It's alright. You can come out now. I've sussed it."

"What I wouldn't give to break into television," continued the disembodied voice, "Like the *Mastermind* chair. And she doesn't even speak. Just sits there. Well, is sat upon, really. Looking smug, as if she knows any of the answers."

As the voice bemoaned its lot, Tony scanned the waiting room for hidden cameras or concealed microphones but could see nothing untoward. Obviously, the speaker could be hidden inside the chair's substantial padding.

"Or the *BBC Breakfast* sofa," continued the voice, wistfully, "All those celebrities and sports personalities ..."

"Look here," interrupted Tony, "I know it might spoil your programme and that, but ... I've found you out. You can come out now." Tony moved towards the window. Perhaps the cameras were outside somewhere? Or across the street? Tony twizzled the stick that closed the Venetian blinds. That would stop their little game. As he looked expectantly towards the door, the chair let out an exaggerated sigh.

"Phewwwer ..."

Tony crossed to the waiting-room door, edging it open just enough to poke his head through the gap. He surveyed the corridor in both directions for any sign of TV hosts or directors or whatever. There was a distinct absence of activity.

"So, what do I do now?" he asked aloud.

"I'm sorry. Are you talking to me?" The chair sounded slightly sarcastic.

"Of course I'm talking to you. There's no one else here," Tony spluttered, then realised, "What am I doing?! I'm talking to a chair!"

"Yes ... well ... as you say ... there's no one else here."

"But chairs don't talk!" Tony was getting frustrated with himself.

"No ... most of them don't bother," the voice mused morosely, "Fed up with being ignored, I suppose. But my back was playing up. I don't suppose you could give me a bit of a rub, could you? Across the shoulders."

"No, I ... What the ...? Chairs don't talk!" Tony was getting more and more exasperated.

"I'll remind myself of that next time my back is playing up and I'm feeling depressed. Not that it does any good," the chair complained gloomily, adding hopefully, "Just a little rub?"

"I'm sorry if I was a bit ... short-tempered," Tony apologised as he stepped cautiously behind the chair. "It's just that I've never ... well ... you know."

"What's so odd about a talking chair?" queried the chair, "Other stuff talks, doesn't it?"

"No, other stuff *doesn't* talk," Tony explained calmly, as if to a child. Almost without thinking, he had begun to massage the leather at the top of the chair's buttoned back. The action was having a calming effect on Tony as much as it appeared to be relieving the chair's stress.

"Down a bit, if you don't mind," the chair directed him with a deep sigh. "What about phones? Everybody talks to them all the time. And radios. And televisions."

"That's different," said Tony, "That's technology."

"Speak-your-weight machines!" There was a modicum of doubt in the chair's claim. "Do they still have those?"

"I don't know. I don't think so," confessed Tony, "I've only ever seen them in American films."

"And sat-navs! What about sat-navs?!" declared the chair triumphantly, then continued appeasingly, "Though I will admit you don't get a proper conversation with a sat-nav."

To Tony's amusement, the chair's tone of voice took on a slightly robotic quality as it mimicked a passable impression of a sat-nav. "In one hundred yards, turn left. In two hundred yards, turn right. Turn around where possible. It's not exactly a commentary on the scenery or a guide to the best place to get a cappuccino. It's just bossy back-seat driving. Not even a proper front seat. They have a very limited vocabulary. *You have reached your destination*? Huh! Still ... I suppose it's an apposite paradigm of the human condition."

"What?!" exclaimed Tony, somewhat taken aback by this strange conversational tangent.

"Thinking you know where you are when you have no idea how you got there," explained the chair, "It makes a mockery of all the advances in existential thinking."

"Yes, I suppose it does," Tony admitted dubiously.

"Do you really agree?" the chair asked mournfully, "or are you just saying that to appease me ... because I'm a chair."

"No, truly, I think you're right," said Tony, "If we gave more thought to our life's journey ... where we'd come from, what had influenced us, what we'd done along the way ... Maybe, I don't know ... Maybe we'd show a bit more humility ... Tolerate the failings of others ..."

"Yes, yes," agreed the chair with a modicum of enthusiasm, "People might see the essence of the individual and not just the labels that were attached to them along the way."

"Like nationality and gender and race ..." Tony was warming to the subject.

"And chair," interjected the chair. "Maybe the people who come in here would realise that I am me – not just a chair."

Tony sensed that there was a gentle but implicit rebuke tucked away behind this argument.

"Yes ... well ... I suppose, when I first heard you talk, I was as much at fault as any of them. Only ... I've never heard a chair speak before."

"Have you ever stopped to listen?" There was still a hint of rebuke in the chair's tone.

Tony just shook his head, as if listening to chairs was one of those things that you were actually meant to do. Like cleaning your teeth before bedtime. Or taking your litter home with you. Or holding doors open for people pushing buggies.

There was an awkward silence while Tony tried to frame his next query in a way that would not cause offence.

"If you don't mind me asking," Tony ventured cautiously, "How come you can speak?"

"Hmmmm," the chair sighed thoughtfully, "You know the question you ought to be asking is not *How can a chair speak?* but *How did I get to be a chair?* It's what I ask myself all the time."

"And ...?" Tony let the question hang in the space between himself and this philosophical piece of furniture. He presumed that the chair was thinking - though, in the absence of body language or facial expression, he could not be sure. He risked a prompt.

"So ... have you always been a chair?"

"Oh ... you don't listen, do you?" sighed the chair, "I told you ... It's what I've become."

"Yes, yes ..." Tony was eager to show that he was being attentive, "What I meant was .. what were you before you were a chair?"

"I'm not entirely sure," replied the chair, "It's all a bit hazy ... Does that sound absurd?"

"I suppose life is absurd, isn't it?" Tony reflected.

"Oh, oh," the chair was suddenly animated, if one can use that term about a piece of furniture, "I remember ... I was Visiting Chair of Philosophy at ... Some University or Other. Place names don't really matter, whatever the sat-navs say. It's what you do along the way and when you get there that counts."

"So ... what did you do?" Tony sought elucidation.

"Oh, you know. The usual stuff. To do is to be. To be is to do. Do be do be do. How they laughed. Not. Cats in boxes. Trees in forests. One hand clapping. If this is a question, what's your answer? All of that stuff. Now look at me. Just part of the furniture in a psychiatrist's waiting room. Apprehensive about talking to strangers."

"Chary, you might say," Tony risked the pun.

"Yes," the chair half-chuckled, "Anyway, thanks for the conversation. Better than talking to the clock. You'd think he'd have at least a rudimentary understanding of the space-time continuum. But no. Just ticking off the minutes 'til his batteries run down."

Tony glanced up at the clock, which he imagined turned to look in a different direction; not keen to join the conversation. Anyway, there were only a few minutes to go before his appointment. "And the massage," said the chair, remembering, "Thanks for the massage. I'm just going to ... you know ..."

"Yeah, of course," Tony conceded, "Best ..."

Tony patted the chair consolingly: stroked its high leather back with a degree of tenderness. Then he crossed the waiting room and planted himself gently on a brightly-coloured, retro-plastic chair with tubular-metal legs, which he imagined winced slightly under his weight. Picking up the copy of *Cosmopolitan* from the coffee table, he turned the pages until he found the questionnaire.

Is penis size related to the size of a guy's feet? it asked.

John Fewings

RECLAIMING THE LANDSCAPE

I

He locks his hands
around a mug of tea,
describes morning's steep walk
past boarded-up shops
to his mother's Care Home.

He remembers the town
from childhood –
just one street
since the colliery closed
though saplings flourish
on slag heaps,
green them year by year
into wooded hills.

And his mother?

He shakes his head.

II

It's July, nineteen-fifty one.
She's forty weeks pregnant
and craves sweet blue fruit.
She kicks off her sandals,
turns, waves, throws them
to her husband.
She's laughing   running
scaling the mountain
                behind her house,
plucking fistfuls
                of ripe wimberries,
cramming them
                into her mouth.

Sheila Jacob

MAY YOU BE AS DIFFICULT AS YOUR BROTHERS
(after reading A Prayer for My Daughter by W B Yeats and Born
Yesterday by Philip Larkin)

Fetching you from your cot I watch you wake,
stand, rattle the bars desperate to be out.
Like the fabled fairy I wish you health and heart,
but not in any wand-waving way.

May you be as beautiful as you like,
preen if you want to, not forgo
the pleasures of good looks for the sake
of superficial suitors, but learn

to recognise them, steer clear,
save yourself the bother of fragile egos.
If that can't be managed, may you be
resilient to their vitriol.

Out-with the bounds of human kindness don't
temper your demeanour for others or
let selflessness run too much towards
self-sacrifice and desire to please.

May you be your own best friend;
be sane and sensible – with flair;
only seem ordinary, dull
to those blind to a lofty mind.

May you flourish in full view, not hidden,
take time to choose your dear perpetual place,
only take root when it suits.

Ann Gibson

FIREWORKS
(After Charles Dickens: A Tale of Two Cities)

She resented him with particular animosity
when she left the dinner table to watch
the bonfire-night fireworks in the garden

of their Victorian semi, packed and tight.
But it was a happy house. Happier at least
than the ones that followed. Did she really think

walls, bricks or ceilings had anything
to do with it? No – it was more about the way
he enraged her by emptying the understair

cupboard into a steaming pile of wellies,
coats-for-all-seasons, odd gloves and all
the paraphernalia of a life spent raising

small children. She thought she would divorce
him over this but never said the words aloud.
Five years later, those small frustrations

never voiced, those tears that wouldn't fall
at the disappointment of it all, those red dots
that appeared all over her soft skin as a cruel

reminder of her own mortality. Five years later,
one of the things she resented with particular
animosity was shaving over the bald patch

on his head in the crumbling bathroom
of their hired apartment in a foreign city.
A reminder of his own mortality.

She remembered as a child she would
check the back of her old dad's head,
but he never did lose a hair even when

he had lost everything else. The fireworks
had excited her but he could only look on
resentfully at the dirty knives and forks.

Natalie Fry

THE TALE OF A NORTHERN FISHWIFE

Down under the pier, where custard foam
jostles used condoms and sporks like pearls;
that's where he found her; *they say, she says.*
She was dancing in a chip-wrapper veil
but nowt else, she and a friend,
blue breasted and chaffed.

He says as they saw him approach through the spit:
one grabbed her skin from the dunes, changed
into to a black-eyed seal and swam away.
He snatched the second pelt, slick and fatty,
tucked it into his belt before the other could reach it.
Reeled her in with a squeal, led her home naked;
they say, he says.

From a saucy flotsam he took her to wife,
and they bought a seaside B&B called The Mermaid.
She bore him two sons; *they said, they said,*
all pale flat eyes, cold scaly-skinned.
She had their names tattooed on her backside
with a picture of a bucket and spade, *they said.*

She loved her husband as well as she could,
but each second Tuesday she ran, *they said,*
down to the beach, ate a 99, reclined
in a stripy deckchair and stared and waited,
stared out at the vast grey slate.

He told the officers, she'd been on her knees
counting canned cockles, boxes of fish sticks.
He assumed, she found that loose floorboard,
under the stairs, *he said, he said.*
Must've found that old coat of hers,
all bright, briny and barnacled,
that he'd hidden away for past twenty years.

She ran and was gone just like that
no turning back; *he said, he said.* Put on her old life
over the new and swam away and away,
away. He looked and looked, but there was no trace,
he said. He looked and he looked, *so they say.*

Jennie E Owen

FAMILY REUNION

In theory, it's what you want the most
at least in part. Convened by one unseen
for years, not missed; but any chance to see
the family together in one room
is something precious, something to await

and here it is: you look across the board
and see the faces you once saw each day
now older, like the running jokes and tropes
that still evoke familiar laughs and groans.

The factions reconvene, rôles re-emerge
– the leader, clown, the sniper on the side
– there's needling, but baits are bitten back
and you catch looks as history replays.

But time is short – you're barely warming up
you've hardly thought of things you want to say –
when someone's leaving and the bill's been paid.
With hugs and shaken hands we shuffle out

and after all the build-up we disperse
to separate silos where we live our lives
to be debriefed perhaps, or think alone
about the highlights, how it's come to this.

Stuart Handysides

His mother's eyelid droops. Will his? He's in the bathroom mirror. Washing half-blind, he discovers the skin on the inside of his wrist and nothing should be so delicate.

He's standing over her. Female smells fill the dark room. Steakish smells. His daughter sleeps like fog. He rushes to the window for a drink of light. He goes back to her. Her chin line is a piece of thread. If he touched it, she might cease to be, to have ever been. Her floor is covered in outfits. Some of them meet. He steps away, already cross at the day. But he mustn't fail her. He is her day. He suddenly wants good things and he's back at the window tearing open curtains and lifting the old window that gasps on its rail. Oh, why does she remember the bad stuff? Like him making that boy cry by joking about his moles. What about the cuddles? The world must be full of lost gestures. To be among them is sometimes his only aspiration. He returns to her. We're striking out, he says. You and me. Her smile is a baby's. Last night's laughter is in her hair. Where did she go? Her new smile is tight. Striking out, he repeats. Then walks to the door, which he opens. Then he's at the top of the stairs. He doesn't believe in downstairs; all faith has left him. The passageway is a picture. Too narrow for a normal soul. It can't possibly hold life, or anything tall. He calls out that he is going down. Sheets whisper and a weight shifts. He goes down. The passageway rises to meet him.

If only he could get her into a different air. Shovelfuls of it she needed. The furniture tenses. He sits at the table and soothes its seats, its crockery, its lined tablecloth. Sunshine leans on the window, reaches in to touch the cutlery. The air is happy. Hope is a downstairs feeling. And now his legs bend, feet turning in and back and coiling round the chair legs. His arms halve for elbows and he rests his head in his palms. On the mantle-piece sits a bowl of pink hyacinths just out of bulbs. And now she is here, as if she had no need of stairs.

'I could eat a peach,' she says and the fruit word gives her colour. As she puts herself down, he gets up, and the see-saw moment produces a lurch. In the kitchen, he finds a peach. Rushes back. Ah, she is still there. He sits off to one side and the angle makes her realer. She gazes at the peach, picks it up. She is in a white top, pale yellow bottoms. Her feet are bare. Her toes grip the floor and then the limbs of the chair that go across. He has a horror of feet, which aren't very different from hands, whose palms can be as yellow, as reptilian. The lines travel this way and that too, your destiny is the same.

'I've set aside the day for you,' he says, but she is into her peach. Her head threatens to come away and fruit blood, thin and watery, flings itself down her chin. 'The day,' he reminds.

'You can't earmark a day,' she says. 'It's not yours.'

'It was something to say,' he says and thinks, *Give me a mouse to speak to and some dust to hide it.*

'That's your trouble,' she says. 'How you say a thing occludes what you're saying.' Her eyes flash, her jaw tenses, her teeth sharpen on him. *A mouse, a mouse.*

'I'm sorry,' he says. And she relents, shrinks in her chair and the peach, still in her hand, grows. One side eaten.

'Your thumbprint is all over me,' she says.

His eye gets trapped in the tablecloth check.

She places the back of a cereal spoon against her left eye. The eye must be open. He picks up his spoon, it's heavy, its silver is greenish, but before he can react, she snatches it from him to hold up to the other eye, so that she is blind. Laughing, she removes the spoons and there is no sign of blink. She notices the hyacinths and asks about bulbs that come to nothing. Too sad to reply, he rises to put the kettle on, set some bread under the grill.

When he's back, the peach is over. She looks hopefully at the teapot as he sails it. The steam is lost on the air. When the teapot is still, the steam ringlets. He leaves and returns with toast. Pouring and buttering happen easily.

'I'm too tired,' she says. She is a heap of bones.

'I wanted something for you,' he said. He'd prepared a couple of thoughts for the walk. *The privilege of passing under a tree.* And: *I'd like to own a single bird outright.*

'I know, but I'm tired,' she said. 'Little movements tire me. I'm almost happy. The peach has been a sort of life highlight. But now I need to rest.'

Look at the garden, he longs to say. His arm goes to move, but the impulse is cut off at the wrist. The garden waits, though as he stares the path narrows and the flowers, flirting in the breeze, stiffen and choke on their sap. A white cat watches him, understanding everything, doing nothing.

'The garden?' he says hopelessly.

'I can't move for you,' she says with her head turned away. A neck tendon, pulled into prominence, expresses more. 'Your thoughts are everywhere.'

Anger is touched off, his cheeks burn.

'You were such a joyful child.'

'Not that, please,' she says, facing him. Her eyes brighten, dull. 'Anything but the past. You don't get it. Or won't. It isn't there. It never was. It hasn't happened yet. It might not.'

Simon Howells

We all remember where we were
when we heard. I'm taken back
to our back room in Ballydowd,
nearly bedtime, playing with my doll,
Jacqueline, named for his wife.

My mother, forlorn, doleful
at the divine contrivance
that Peter Lawford, his brother-in-law,
Sinatra's key man in the White House,
should be on telly as the news broke.

In June I'd seen him wave from his motorcade
across the river, us on the top deck of the Lucan bus
on Aston's Quay, me bemused by the fuss;
emperor's new clothes, and that before
his clay feet were bared.

These memories sparked in a different century,
by a fourpenny pattern in a pile my mother left;
creased, stained with a few drops of spilt tea,
for a Lady's Raglan Sweater with Collar
in Mahoney's Killowen Double Knit or Blarney Fleck.

Being all-the-rage retro, I opened it,
and in her old-school penmanship,
along the top, a message
brought her here; 'I was knitting this
the night JF Kennedy was shot'.

Ann Gibson

PLAYING CARDS WITH MY MOTHER

How long since the sea pulled up its roots,
trees choked, cars began to bounce
across the water, crusted over now?
You hesitate over diamonds,
spread them out, slightly grubby,
stiffening on your fingertips.

I learn next day why the bank –
a horrid letter –
wanted to check.
It was the online subscription –
asking you questions –
for continence pads.

I always liked the clubs.
You run the numbers: 7, 9,
8, 10. Your granddaughter
puts her hand near yours,
deftly straightens and moves.
The tree won't fall.

Your voice is calm –
you say you've never played
before. I'm watching your hands
and mine, the diamonds twisting
along our fingers, the electric light.

Carolyn Oulton

Within a month or two of each other they were both gone. My parents. I feel as though I should be sad, but if I'm honest I'm not. Not really. They had both had long lives. Mostly happy, but not completely so. Everyone needs some bad to know how good the good times are. They had avoided the fearful hydra of dementia and in the end just passed away in their sleep. They were in their late nineties. People call that a good innings, which I suppose is true, unless you're the one facing the last ball of the over. There is a bench by the sea on the east coast I like to sit on and enjoy the view on a late summer evening. The bench is dedicated to someone called George Entwhistle who had in 1994 'Gone out with the tide'. For my parents it was a similar gentle but unstoppable ebbing away.

There was only me left to clear up the remains of two lives. I had a brother in New Zealand, but he'd gone over there with his girlfriend some sixty years earlier as a young man and was now just too damn old and broke to make the long journey back to the UK. In any case, he'd left under a cloud – one of the not so good times – after a series of blazing rows with my father over something or other. My brother was a bit older than me so I never learned what. He'd never been back and we didn't really keep in touch. I told him about our parents by email.

I went round to their bungalow to go through things and see if there was anything I wanted to keep before I had the house cleared and sold.

As you'd expect, there was nothing much. Everything had worn out, was tattered, battered, grubby and useless. Anything vaguely useful would have been a duplicate of a better one I already had. The photos faded in their frames; I already had digital versions of all of them. The total net worth of the rest of the stuff, mostly dark brown furniture, coat hangers and tired bedding was the cost of a large skip. I found a few old letters, a few postcards, a ribbon tied round a lock of blond hair. My father's Timex watch, which had long since stopped working and was yellow-faced and slightly rusty. There was the usual collection of walking sticks, zimmer frames, teach-beak cups, sticks for grabbing stuff you can't reach, toenail clippers, magnifying glasses and plastic spectacles. A vast array of daily medications laid out in serried ranks of plastic dose dividers. Musty, old, thin, worryingly stained bedding, a commode, a great deal of fluff, an ancient tin of salmon, a twenty year old raspberry jelly conjoined with its plastic wrapper and that curious smell that old people's houses get from goodness know what.

It was all a bit depressing and in truth, I just wanted it over and done with. I wanted to get to the end of the chapter, close the book and get on with the business of my own ebbing away.

Then I found the bundle of letters in a shoe box. Well, actually it was a box for a pair of flower-patterned velour ladies slippers. Size 4. My mum was a size 6 and favoured slip-ons and these were the full slipper. The top letter was addressed to my dad and was dated almost thirty years ago. It said, simply, 'It's over. Leave me alone. Don't contact me anymore. Here are your letters. I hope you're happy with your other wife. Goodbye. Daphne.' A single x for a farewell kiss. Time was getting on, so I took the box home with me. By telephone I called down the circling vultures - the estate agents, the house clearance specialists, the council, the gas and electric, the TV licence. All that tedious, depressing unravelling of lives no longer lived. By the evening I was so thoroughly fed up with it all I just unwound with a gin and tonic of truly epic proportions and went to bed early.

The next day I pulled out the stack of letters and began to go through them. Within the first two sides it was clear that my father had been carrying on a clandestine extra marital affair with a woman called Daphne, that the affair had gone on for more than fifty years, that Daphne had always looked forward to my father finally settling down when he retired from work. It also transpired that Daphne and my father had long ago had a child, a girl called Chloe, who must be about my age. Most of the letters were just everyday stuff, the boring catalogue of a travelling salesman's wanderings around his patch and of the woman who waited and kept a home for him. Of their daughter's growing up and eventual elopement. Of two lives lived apart for days or weeks at a time. Until the end, when Daphne's heart was broken. Broken when my father finally owned up to being married to a different woman whom he would never leave. Needless to say, my father had never spoken of this, not to me at any rate.

There was an address, so fishing out my largely unused senior citizen's bus pass I caught a bus, found the house and, with some trepidation knocked on the door.

The door was answered by a woman in jeans and sweatshirt holding a loud baby. I introduced myself and asked if Daphne still lived there, only to find that Daphne was long dead and the woman had bought the house from the people who had bought it originally from Daphne's estate. I went home. I was feeling pretty hollow, flat and limp.

Out of the blue my brother called.

"Mate," he said. His New Zealand accent, still, strangely, touched with a hint of Barnsley. "I've got some bad news."

"OK," I said, "I've got some news too, but you first."

"Mate," he stopped for a moment and I could hear the wavering, the catch in his voice. I knew it was serious.

"What is it John," I said, gently.

"It's the wife, Chloe," he said, "she died in her sleep last night. Heart. I thought you might want to know."

I was silent for a moment. A moment longer than a heartbeat. "I'm sorry to hear that John, is there anything I can do?" I knew, as people always do, that there was nothing I could do.

"No mate. Gemma is devastated to have lost her mum of course, but she's here with me now. I just wanted to let you know. We've been together all this time. Ever since we came over here on the SS Maui Pomare. It won't seem right without her." He paused and I let the pause hang. "What was your news?" he asked.

I thought for a moment.

"Oh, nothing," I said, "nothing that matters now."

Steve Dalzell

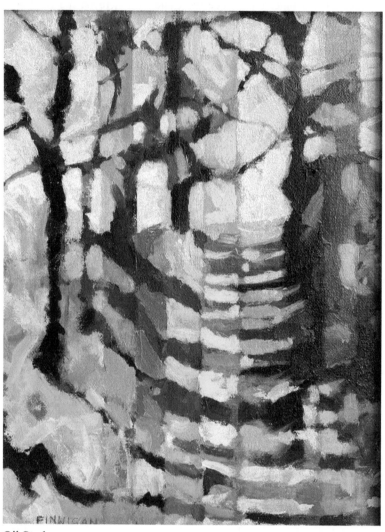

Oil Study

'I'm not asking much now am I? Not in turn for the farm, this house.'
He staggered towards the chair, creasing into its greasy seat. As if in
punctuation he indicated to the four yellowing walls in turn with his stick.
'I don't want the farm, you know I don't...'
'Sell it then, use the money on those spoilt grandchildren I've never met.'
His eyes were wide and red rimmed, she did not know whether it was
through fear or anger – she never had.
'Dad...'
'Burn the place down then, I don't care what you do. I just don't want
to be here to see the flames, nor the smile on your face as you toss in the
match.'
She turned her back on him and walked out of the parlour, out of the
shows of the farm house, she would have kept on walking right out of his
life, if it hadn't have set its own too rapid pace by then.
She stopped at the gate and found she couldn't bear to turn back around
to look at the house; the house in which she had been dragged up for plenty
long enough to know that farming wasn't for her. It repelled her. Yet, here
she was, once again.
She knew he would never let her forget what a disappointment she was
to him, even more so than Barbara. Barbara and Jay had run to the other
side of the World, but at least they were still working the land on their farm
in New Zealand. She'd noticed a photo of her sister and her two freckled
children on the otherwise empty mantle when she'd arrived.
In front of her the fields lay empty, green and picturesque. They should
be speckled as far as the eye could see by the black and white flanks of the
herd, but here they were, deserted. The scent of cows must have been
coming from the ground itself. Twenty miles of rolling hills stood between
the farm and the nearest town. Behind her, just her father and a whole load
of ill feeling.
She could see the appeal as she stood there in the June sun allowing
herself to imagine just for a moment the boys playing and laughing in the
pasture. It was beautiful, on the surface at least. She thought of the typical
image of a dairy farm, cows and calves feeding happily in the open air.
She knew it was a good job most people didn't know how they had to be
made pregnant over and over, how the male calves were taken away within
hours to the back barn with a bolt gun. She had hated calving most of all.
And now there was this thing, this new final thing he was asking of her.
Unthinkable. And yet she knew what it must have cost him and his pride
to call her all the way back here to talk to her; back to the empty farm
where he was now just a bent and broken king with no court. She thought
about all the changes, not to the farm that had always been dilapidated, but
to the man himself. The man she once thought was formed out of rope and

tight knots seemed to have uncoiled. He had begun to forget things, where he had left his stick, his pipe. He hadn't even mentioned her mother once in all of this. How it was her fault he'd been left alone with two ungrateful children – girls to boot.

The only thing she had loved about living on the farm growing up was the freedom to explore the countryside, the woodland and the river. She and Barbara had spent hours just walking when they were kids, navigating pot holes; taking off socks and shoes and paddling the slippery stones on the river bed. Then when they were older they spent evenings trying to walk and hitch rides away to the village. Barbara soon got pulled into the farming, whilst she had always been too young, too small, too good at getting under foot to be of any real help.

One particular summer she had spent in the top field going hungry and getting burnt, playing mother to a litter of wild kittens that had made their home in the top rafters of an old stone cottage. She would ignore the scratches, feeding them scraps of meat she had taken from the kitchen or the dog's bowls. She'd even slept one or two nights up there when the sky was clear, and still no one seemed to have noticed. Not even Barbara, who she shared a room with, had made comment.

She traced the shrunken perimeter of the farm by eye. Jay had done a good job of the fencing, she could see that, it was mostly dry wall and some hedging. It had all been barbed wire when she was a child. She still had scars behind her right knee from where she'd been chased by the bull and got caught clambering over the top to get to the next field.

Finally with reluctance she turned and looked back at the house. Two of the upstairs windows had cracked and were now lined with cardboard. The third, her father's, was wide open. It had always been that way, even in the winter when you would wake to frozen pipes and your breath a freezing fog above the bedsheets. She still couldn't quite understand how she had survived her infancy. She supposed one of the local women had come to help look after her; either that or her father's stories about leaving her in the pig pen to be raised by Big Martha had more truth in them than she wanted to imagine.

As soon as she was eighteen, she'd left a note and gone to University. She hadn't even told Barbara she was applying, she'd asked the school to help with the forms. Because of this she knew she couldn't be angry that she'd only found out about her sister's marriage years later. Barbara and Jay had stuck around for a bit by all accounts to help her father, but she expected the other side of the world had got appealing for them both really quickly.

Her thoughts flickered back to the kittens and the summer she played mother cat. She didn't want to think about that again, especially not now; but it was as if she kept searching out the memory in her mind, like a tongue worrying over a broken tooth.

She had been reluctantly making her way back from the cottage, driven finally to the house by hunger. When she'd heard a faint cry of distress; she remembered thinking that for a moment it was her own. Then she saw something moving and saw it was one of the kittens, now four or five weeks old. What it was doing this far from its home she did not know. She bent to gather it in her arms but in the dusk half-light she found it caught on the wire, its rear legs tangled and bleeding. There was a smell of rust. She carefully untangled the wire and the kitten; it was the tabby and white male she had called Nevin after the village vet. It barely moved. She took off her cardigan, the blue oversized one that had been her mother's, and gathered it into her arms. There was a bad smell coming from the legs and at least one looked broken. It mewed pitifully. She walked back to the house with it cradled like a baby, hushing and shushing the way she thought mothers must.

Instead of going through the kitchen door where she would find no kindness, she had made her way around to the back of the house where the feed was prepared. There in a bucket full of lukewarm water she took the kitten gently and held it under the surface, watching the bubbles escape its lungs with red curling. It hardly struggled. It took only a moment and the kitten had gone from a living thing to a nothing. At most a piece of meat. She looked up and saw her father watching from the back window, he seemed to be half smiling over his pipe. He turned away and back into the room, which had become the brightest square of light in the evening darkness. She wiped the tears from her eyes on the sleeve of her shirt and buried the kitten, still wrapped in her mother's clothes in the corner of the yard in a shallow grave; where no doubt the foxes dug it up later.

The sky was blue, unbroken and like a solid thing. She felt as though everything was slightly unreal; the farm merely a set from her childhood that had been overlooked when everything else had been dismantled. She took a deep breath and tried not to think of the boys at home with Greg. She tried to forget her job, her life, the world outside this static memorial she was trapped inside.

She pushed open the front door with a creak and stepped over the stone where her father had sharpened the knives. Under her skin she felt warm water and damp fur.

Jennie E Owen

VIRTUES AND PERFECTIONS: MARY TUDOR MEETS KING PHILIP OF SPAIN
(Hampton Court, Autumn 1554)

I

He kissed me on the mouth, English fashion.
I breathed the down of his skin, the silk warmth
of his beard. We stood together, held hands,
spoke French or Spanish, used the language
of Holy Mother Church if words faltered.
I taught him to say Goodnight, my Lords all.
He thanked me for the jewelled suits, tailored
to fit his slender hips, and I knew then,
at last, how it was to desire a man,
yearn for his body in my marriage bed.
I burned through the pain, caressed his damp hair
when he quivered, cried out then slipped from me.
He slept soundly, afterwards; woke first light
to hear Mass. I dozed, prayed I had pleased him.

II

These nights, between lavender-scented sheets,
in the soft half-dark of our bedchamber,
I forget I was eleven years old
when he was born. White hair turns silver-red,
falls across my breasts. He presses his lips
to mine. I clasp my hands around his neck,
yield to him eagerly as wife, woman,
queen; find so many virtues and perfections
I rejoice, dance until my cheeks glow pink.
A true Tudor rose, my waiting-ladies
smile, though I am Catherine's daughter, too.
Pomegranate seed, pomegranate fruit.
I retched yesterday, before breakfast, craved
the bitter-sweet flesh of unripe apples.

Sheila Jacob

ON CORONATION DAY
(In remembrance)

She couldn't easily have removed it
unaware that a thin green caterpillar was
inching along the shoulder of her gown,
its front feet clinging to the white satin
while the body gathered itself into a loop –
an exclamatory O – before its head
reached one earring and, in Os after Os,
made for the jewel on the Princess's head.

A *Pieris rapae* – cabbage white butterfly –
a pest which eats almost anything and hides
on the midrib of leaves or a *Trichoplusia ni,*
another pest which will give life to a cabbage
looper moth? Hard to tell, now it's perched
on George IV State Diadem where the creature,
standing upright, raised its head as if whiffing
the air of Pall Mall through the roof of the royal
coach slowly gliding towards Westminster.

Under the gothic vaulting of the Abbey
the caterpillar sensed the alienation of the place
and crawled on a wisp of hair of the royal head.

We shall never know whether the larva came
to adulthood: cabbage white or looper moth
or was diplomatically crushed between the
ringed fingers of the archbishop, since both have
died and the Princess has been changed
                                        into a Monarch.

Marie Papier

The spot is marked by a 12-foot obelisk composed of lava rocks. Melted earth. The area of the crater is surrounded by a barbed wire fence. In one direction is a mountain wall. The rest of the landscape is barren desert. A truly remote location. After more than 75 years, the area is still slightly radioactive.

Before Hiroshima, before Nagasaki, there was Trinity. On the morning of July 16, 1945, the world's first nuclear device was exploded in the remote desert of New Mexico. As the morning sky was rent by the explosion, J. Robert Oppenheimer recalled the lines from the Bhagavad Gita – "Now I am become Death, the destroyer of worlds."

It was a destination I knew I would have to visit in my travels. I would have to stand in the spot where the human animal, unique among the beasts, had become capable of causing its own extinction.

I stopped in Socorro, New Mexico, about thirty miles northwest of the Trinity site. In a roadside diner, I met an old timer who had been alive at the time of the blast. He told me about the night it had occurred, when the sky was a bath of white and the sound of thunder had come tearing across the desert. A few weeks later he heard about Hiroshima and Nagasaki and knew what that night had wrought.

He spoke of going to the Trinity Site as a child and collecting strange chips of stone, altered by the blast, a substance that would later be called trinitite. Then the government had arrived and cordoned off the area. He related tales of protesters who occasionally came with signs, protesting the atomic bomb, or wars, or nuclear power, or the use of the bomb at Hiroshima, or Trinity itself. And he said the people of his generation had suffered "a lot of ailments" through the years, from living so close to the bomb site. But it never occurred to him to move. This was his home. This was all he knew. To him, an atom bomb might go off in your neighborhood when you're a child. It's just a part of life.

The Trinity Site is deep inside the White Sands Missile Base. I had to pass through a barbed-wire gate and show photo identification. I was told to drive about 17 miles down a desert road until I came to the Permanent High Explosive Testing Area. I was then to turn left. I was worried I might miss the turn, but there was no chance of that. When I reached the fork in the road, an armed soldier stood sentry, making certain I didn't accidentally stray into the Permanent High Explosive Testing Area. He didn't feel half as strongly about it as I did.

After driving another five miles, I could see the obelisk in the distance, surrounded by a large, circular barbed wire fence, the size and shape of the blast crater. I had to exit my car and pass on foot through another guarded gate.

I stood where Oppenheimer had stood, and Fermi and Teller. There were those who had chosen not to come, like Leo Szilard, who did not want to witness what they had done.

In the final days before the detonation, a macabre humor had developed among the scientists. They had organized a betting pool to predict the size of the explosion. General Groves received disturbing reports from the Army guards – Enrico Fermi was taking side bets on whether they would accidentally ignite the atmosphere and end all life on the planet.

The device was placed on a metal grate tower with wires leading to various measuring devices. The scientists set it off just before dawn.

It has been called "The Day the Sun Rose Twice."

An atomic tourist who looks carefully on the ground can still see examples of trinitite, a substance that doesn't exist anywhere else in the world. It was created when the nuclear explosion fused the desert sand of New Mexico. A piece of trinitite is about a centimeter wide. The top surface is smooth and green. The bottom is light gray and rough and looks like concrete. The most common form of trinitite is green, but there is also black, red, and blue. Black trinitite contains occlusions of iron from the tower which held the device. Red trinitite is caused by the fusing of copper from the wires that were run from the bomb to the various measuring devices. No one knows what causes blue trinitite. It is illegal to remove a piece of trinitite from the area. All trinitite is radioactive.

After absorbing enough history, and probably more than enough radiation, I got back into my car and headed toward the state highway, glad to leave the Trinity site in my rearview mirror.

H.G. Wells, one of history's seminal thinkers, had thought the tank so horrific – as it rolled insensate across the bodies of dead and wounded soldiers and civilians, as it destroyed fields, and ruined villages – that the world would be unable to face the horrors of such a monstrous weapon and would be forced to put an end to war once and for all. The thinkers of an earlier generation had believed the same thing about the rapid-fire Gatling gun. The next generation would hold the same belief about the atomic bomb.

I imagine that somewhere in our dim, dark past, a cave philosopher noticed that the attacking tribe was swinging sticks, and thought, *"Ann Gibson Simon Howells Stuart Handysides,* this can't go on!"

After making his name and fortune writing prophetic tales of science fiction, H.G. Wells turned his great mind to anti-war activism and spent the latter part of his life trying to save the world.

He didn't realize the world doesn't want to be saved.

When the earliest human discovered he had an opposable thumb, the first thing he made was a fist.

Mark Pearce

STRAYS

Sitting on the back doorstep of 27 Booth Street –
that's where I first saw them; two beautiful stray boys
drying themselves off after a cold shower
in that pummelling Sydney summer of 1988.
One was brown with cormorant black dreadlocks
and pockmarked skin like my own, yet brightened by irreverence;
the other Maasai, tall and thin, with a slender neck
and something remote in his hooded eyes.
No doubt there was a hint of disapproval
for their midday nakedness in my clipped 'excuse me,'
as I stepped between their sycamore key footprints
and beaded bodies into that L-shaped, weatherboard house.
This was my sanctuary, but the people who had taken me in
had moved on, leaving me to somehow fend for myself.
Later, as the sun was going down, the silent one climbed
onto the roof in an orange sarong and serenaded
whatever he saw up there on his conga drum,
while Dreadlocks and his Lioness girlfriend took over
the kitchen, laughing – operatically, it seemed to me.
'Oh, what are they laughing about all the time in that kitchen!'
I remember thinking, as I lay on my single bed
in the yellow laundry, nursing my misfortunes.
Eventually I grew hungry and had to go and find out.
Both boys are gone now, into fireflies of unbroken sleep,
and the cool westerly that hauled away their fortunes
for safekeeping; into ghost stations whose names
I can never quite catch, and faraway hot streets
that lie flat on their backs waiting to be sprayed down
by slow-moving yellow water trucks;
into unidentified birdsong, and unreachable islands
of stranded park benches after a river bursts its banks,
and the anecdotal love of the left behind.
Into this poem too, this fingerprint of thought,
in which two beautiful boys sitting quietly
on a doorstep in their birthday suits,
overlooking the oasis of a long vanished garden,
take no longer to dry off in the sun
than it took you to read it.

Mark Czanik

He chose close hold. I thought: *Poor lonely lad,*
dancing the tango in an upstairs room
with an old broad
on a wet Sunday afternoon.
Absurd and sad.

No doubt some simple error had occurred
(so generous the young, and so polite).
He'll not stay long. Unseemly and absurd
this pairing. Yet he held me very tight,
and whispered in my hair such words!
They scorch me still. Absurd. Obscene. *Absurd!*

Should I have stepped away or slapped his face?
This isn't how we dance. It's not allowed!
Or was I grateful just to be embraced?
His young man's body, eloquently hard,
rendered me helpless to resist.
Who would believe me anyway? Absurd!
A woman twice his age. A fantasist!

Was I abuser or abused?
I've never been the one to make a fuss.
I was appalled by our lewd interlude,
and yet I could not bring it to a close.

So we danced on. The rain danced on the roof,
and no one chose to notice or to care.
And he was gone. Since then, no lovely youth
in error or in hope has climbed that stair.

I wonder now if what I really heard
were the crazed whispers of my own desire?
They whisper still. I think they'll drive me mad,
mocking my fallen face and faded hair.
A love-struck pensioner, absurd and sad.

Pamela Scobie

we're in the vortex of the dance.
So slowly swaying, me,
wonderfully naive and you,
pretty blonde, kissing me deep.

The shock, the pride, the
way I ignite for you,
we could be one
kiss starting us for real,

it's sent me spinning but
a treacherous Matt nicks you;
thing is, it's confidence not heart.
We missed you, hissed the lovecats.

Richard Lister

HEATHCLIFF

His wildness, his violence
fight the coward in me.
He came to me in a dream
and I've woken unable to shift him.
I don't bother to shower
throw on yesterday's clothes.

Yet I cravenly cook breakfast
eat politely, wash up after myself.
He barges in, chucks
crockery out of the kitchen door
broods over sharpened knives
thrills to the pulse of electricity.

He wants me to leave,
live out on the moors,
go barefoot, pull herbs from the ground,
catch trout in my fingers.
He wants me to gallop
on unbridled horses,
have sex on someone's grave.

Jean Stevens

Which way home? The way you ran to Tracey's, along the flyover? Or the shortcut by the canal then over the footbridge and through the estate? The light's OK but it'll be dark in half an hour. You don't want your mum fretting, and if you get home after nine, Dad'll only think you've been with a boy. It's got to be the shortcut.

You can't risk a calf strain with the county trials next weekend, so you do some stretches then jog from Tracey's door, trainers clapping over the wet tarmac, red nylon tracksuit flashing past in the windows of the Minis and Ford Cortinas parked along Dore Street.

The down-at-heel town stretches out below in places you've known all your life. The Victorian library. St Mary's steeple. The old gasworks site. Terraced houses with lights on. Terraced houses with lights off, a blue-grey glimmer downstairs as that mournful trumpet signals the end of *Coronation Street*.

You focus on your pace and breathing, but the bridges come to mind. Granddad used to say they were guarded by trolls when you were little. And they still are. Trolls that smoke weed and steal cars. Trolls with dads who have done time. It's their manor when you cross the railway bridge – and Gail Barton is bound to be hanging out somewhere ahead with her gang.

You slow down and walk up its metal grate steps noticing a train scuttling up the line into the twilight, wheels sparking intermittently like a cigarette butt flicked out of a speeding car.

You tread softly. As you near the top, the asphalt of the high-sided walkway comes into view. All clear. You can't see over the sides, so it feels like you're in a tunnel. Halfway across you hear footsteps clunking up the other side. Is it them? You stop, thinking of your escape route back, whether they'd be quick enough to catch you.

An old couple round the corner. Both are wearing heavy overcoats and thick black NHS specs.

"By 'eck," the man wheezes on seeing you. "Wor I wouldn't give for the legs of a young un."

You give a polite smile, unsure how to reply.

"All right luv," he winks as you pass. "Just wotch yersen."

You start running again, down Water Lane, your back warm and moist now. They're bound to be at the footbridge – ready to trip you up, barge into you. You think about going back, but you'd have to overtake the old couple. Which would make you look lost or silly. Or both.

You pass the last streetlight and turn right onto the towpath. The stagnant water has a dank smell. It's years since you were last here, brambling with

Grandma, and the briars have grown into a wire mesh festooned with rotten cigarette packets and used condoms.

Tracey's mum comes back to you from earlier.

"Sure you don't want a lift, Katie?" She checked as Tracey slouched by the door.

"No, it's fine, Mrs F," you demurred, trying to sound adult. "Thank you."

"Or phone your mum? Let her know you're on your way?"

"I'm fine. Really."

But you're not. Darkness is filling the canal as a slight breeze causes the branches to sweep the dishwater sky. You can see bats zig-zagging above the waterway, but the light is murky, hampered by the large mills on the right and the mature trees lining both banks. The place is alien. You shouldn't be here.

Something scutters in the briars. A rat? There must be thousands of them here. What if they all came teeming across the towpath now? What would you do?

Barton returns to mind.

"Why don't you just leave her alone?" you'd protested when she called Tracey a slag that morning.

Immediately, her bulky face was up close and personal in yours.

"And why dunt yer piss off McKenzie?" she waded in. "Just cos your dad 'as two cars, yer think yer better than us, dunt yer?"

Mrs Holroyd had entered the classroom. But out here there's no Mrs Holroyd, no bell to end a fight. Out here it's just dogshit and discarded cans. And you're the system, the state. A target.

Eighty yards ahead is the dull glow of a lamp attached to an old mill. It's the last light before the footbridge, some four hundred yards away. You remember a news story about a nurse who was raped on her way back from a night shift. What if you were attacked? Would anyone hear your shouts? Or bother to do anything?

You run faster. But the path is muddy in places, and only a yard wide. You'd forgotten it was this narrow and can't risk falling in. Besides, the block-stones on the edge of the canal are a good two or three feet above the water. If you fell in, how would you get out?

You look up at the lamp as you pass. Its rusted iron fitting must predate the First World War. For a moment the light blinds you. You stop, blinking to regain your sight, breathing hard. Can't see a thing. Then you hear the scrunch of footsteps on clinker.

You squint into the gloom. Fifty yards ahead is the glowing orange tip of a cigarette. A stocky male figure. He has a mane of dark wavy hair, like a thick-set version of Jim Morrison, and looks vaguely familiar, but maybe this is wishful thinking. You start jogging again – to show no fear – on the inside edge of the path so he can't push you into the water. Your heart is racing.

"Katie!" he hails, about thirty yards away.

You slow down and walk, racking your brains to think who on earth he is.

"It's young Kate, isn't it?" he inquires with an uncertain smile as you draw near.

You stare at him, gobsmacked. It's Carl, Paula's brother. You once cleaned his Norton with her for 50p before he set off in leathers to a T. Rex concert with his biker mates.

He draws the cigarette to his face and takes a drag like some dude in a western.

"Where yer off ter?" He grins as a veil of smoke wafts across his face.

"Oh, I'm just on my way home," you laugh nervously, already red.

"Well, dunt go ter footbridge. There's a load of lads an lasses waitin' for yer."

He flicks some ash towards the canal.

"Just get yersen back onta main road."

"Ah, cheers Carl. See yer."

You turn and head back the way you came, thinking how weedy you sounded, that you've never said *yer* in your life before. But thank God you're avoiding the footbridge and will be returning under streetlights. Though you're going to be in for it when you get back home.

You run back uphill to Tracey's then left onto the main road. The streetlights cover the pavement in a soft yellow pall. You know you should stop at hers and call your mum, but you're moving now like never before. As if you're flowing, not running. And could go on forever.

You laugh. Carl of all people. In the last place you'd expect him to be. He must be seeing a girl on the estate. You think how beautiful she must be and what it must be like on his motorbike – arms clasped around his hulking body, hair streaming behind.

You run on, fists clenched, trainers caked in mud, slowing briefly at the flyover. Sure enough, a gang is at the footbridge, caught in an arc of light from the estate a hundred or so yards to your left. Some girls are leaning over the bridge, a boy is showing off on a rusted Chopper, and another is pissing into the canal.

The next day you're buzzing. Can't wait to go to school. You've been thinking about Carl all night, and have remembered an incident with him the year before. It was the day after Lee Shipton swore he'd kick Paula's head in. You'd just got off the bus when you heard Carl behind.

"Shipton," he beckoned, "I wanna word wi' you. Our kid says yerve threatened 'er. Well, I've got news for yer. If yer lays a finger on 'er I'm gonna come round an sort yer out. Gerrit?"

Lee looked as if he was about to wet himself. He never went near Paula again.

SEVEN YEARS

Seven years might do it,
seven years of silence,
seven years at my age,
an uncharted significance.
I abandoned all stratagem
after seven years of battle,
no longer inspired
to vanquish the absurd.

The seduction garish, insistent,
an addict to futile solutions,
I sought to quell the churning
chaos of human nature,
to restrain our elegant destruction,
the relentless death of permanence –
idealism, my childhood chum,
finally estranged. My regret:
comprehension arrived too slowly.

I shall endeavor (or endure)
seven years of silence,
though an unlikely buddha,
bumbling through karma,
unversed in nirvana.
I shall likely fail. Will this
silence be equally clamorous,
another predictable fixation,

this shut mouth simply
another rickety construct?
Will my lips be lazy fools
or screwed tight, a hatch
holding back a muddy deluge?
My regret: compassion so vital,
arrived too slowly. I wonder
if there will be a quiet life
after seven years of silence.

David Sapp

HOLIDAY ROMANCE

While shrill cicadas serenade
And cockroaches patrol the dripping shower,
A door slams shut. "You bitch!" A woman screams.

Through the shutters a taxi's headlight beams
Illuminate the lateness of the hour
While shrill cicadas serenade our dreams.

There's romance in the air, and yet it seems
One holiday at least is turning sour.
A door slams shut. "You bitch!" A woman screams.

Across the square each stuttering footstep rhymes
With those, once pace behind, of her pursuer
While shrill cicadas serenade our dreams.

They must have come unstuck, her amorous schemes;
That being so, what can she do but glower?
A door slams shut. "You bitch!" A woman screams.

In mirrored shades, next day, the hot sun gleams;
They hide a bruise, his jealousy's bright flower.
While shrill cicadas serenade our dreams
A door slams shut. "You bitch!" A woman screams.

George Jowett

The carriage rackets like a printing press,
sends all I want to say inwards.

I think of how we used to talk: the shape of *yes*
in each other's mouth.

A boy and girl, deaf to all noise, are sculpting
landscapes
        out of rigid air. Their mouths
            are wide as moons.
There's rain
in their fingers, lightning flash,
      jump-cuts –
         eyes listening sharp
              for a language   that flies
by its kite-strings,
hops
         from palm to palm,
loops/unloops
        in gestures
that ink
the white space   around them.

They splash us with their Perseid showers: fracture
the silence that's got us trapped.

My hand reaches for yours
and lays *I need you* lightly on your skin.

Claire Booker

Creeping downstairs at three in the morning,
trying not to wake the silence or trip over the stillness.

Turning on lights is unavoidable and now the shroud is torn,
the walls startled and the furniture looks out of place
– even the potted plant asks what I'm doing.

Standing over the kitchen sink, I hurriedly drink water
– a stranger in another man's dream.

Iain Blair-Brown

ENDEMIC
SEEDS OF
DOUBT

He was a passionate lover
yet a controlling abuser,
especially when his *new man*
veneer dissolved in drink.
Putdowns, hair pulling
and in time, full-on punches,
were visited on me; often
after sex, when I was opened.
Jekyll and Hyde had nothing
on him. A solipsistic toddler
living in a grown man's body.

We parted thirty-one
years ago, acrimoniously.
I left, was frightened he'd come
for me. I knew his appetite
for revenge if ever he was thwarted.
Thankfully, unusually, he let me be.
He'd found some other distraction
and my lungs and limbs relaxed
as I breathed with profound relief.

This Christmas Eve
I chanced upon his obituary.
The author, his fellow learned
professor, pictured someone
else, a good man: modest, clever,
kind and patient. Even after

all this time, I'm prone
to worry. Was it something
about me that made him cruel?
His stranglehold, his gas-lighting,
I'm still trying to shed. Will I
succeed before I too, am dead?

Ceinwen E Cariad Haydon

CONTROL

All the abusers she'd known
were pathetic bastards
now mostly behind concrete
but the coldest, most evil,
not a single charge against him.

Together in a bar one night,
he said: I'm named, apparently
after that Little Corporal
who sacrificed a million souls,
all cannon fodder to his ego.

She saved for driving lessons
but he said he'd take her
anywhere she wished to go.
In the leather dark of his Jaguar
she felt coddled and afraid.

His dad, a war games fanatic,
for him a more personal control.
Sat watching from the wheel
when she went in to work.
There again when she came out.

John Short

I was taught to please, before I was told I was only a tease.
When the word no, was spoken in whispered screams.
I was taught to ask for what I get.
Yet somehow the rest is fair game,
like the rules were written,
by someone who was taught how to take.
While I was taught to never stay out late.
Never lose my friends, on nights, when I dared to go out.
Watch what I wear.
What it says about me, will shape my whole geography.
I learn about space, before school told me about the big bang.
Be home, before it's dark.
Have your keys in your pocket.
Ready ...
I look at the clothes I want to wear in my brother's wardrobe.
Yet do the clothes you tell me to wear, have pockets?
I lock each thought in a locket of torn pictures.
I halve myself.
Yet the me I see is inside out, to the one you taught me growing up.
This impossible journey.
This unimaginable decision
Was already given to me, the day you raised me.
Taught me how to be what society sees
Is a woman.
Is a man underneath,
and I hate the way you teach boys, by teaching girls, to be ready.
Yet here I am, a man.
My body shaped by a doctor's knife.
My body raped to please someone else.
I was shaped by trauma, hiding as fate.
I am a man, and I know different.
Teach your girls that.

Dalton Harrison

Intimacy Coordinator

Never take for granted the sandwiches she brings to your desk.
Cut her hair whenever she asks, but do not attempt the tightrope
of her fringe. Hand him the remote control like a baton
when he comes to sit beside you on the sofa, for that last push
to the evening's summit he must always climb alone.
Remind him with your lips how he is still the hero of your life.

When she asks you to take the stowaway ant she finds
wandering on the kitchen table from the wildflowers you picked
for her, back to where it belongs, do so without question.
Consider how you sometimes feel not unlike that little creature
in a jam jar yourself, as if one day she will spot you drifting
about the house, and have you returned to your rightful place of origin.
Ask her for help with your apron strings.

Refresh the air. Remember the two honey bees you dreamt of
bumping against the bedroom window, who thanked you
when you lifted the sash to let them out. Become caretakers,
memory guardians as you follow one another through
time's kissing gates, but beware the tributaries of the past.
Learn to identify birdsong and be vigilant for drover's waymarks.
Sit together on the upper deck of double-deckers,
the front seat if available. Let the cleansing spring branches
of overhanging trees wash away any dust that has settled between you.

Watch the way the wind plays with the cherry blossoms
and anything else light enough to give itself up.
Try not to forget how what was stolen from your doorstep
was never yours in the first place; how you woke one morning
lifetimes ago to find an angel had simply left it there.

Leave handwritten notes. Be patient with one another's untidiness:
the apple stalks and breadcrumbs under his desk,
the crushed water lilies she drops everywhere.
Read to her in bed, the way you used to. Make love
that is as gripping and real as the last page of a favourite book
you have somehow forgotten the ending of, one you have to slowly
uncover with your fingers, a sentence at a time.

When parting, be like the falling star who feels nothing
as it falls but disappointment that it cannot sit in pride of place
with the moon anymore.

Mark Czanik
Dream Catcher 46

AT THE TANKERY INN
("The music is not in the notes, but in the silence between."
Wolfgang Amadeus Mozart)

The guitars are put aside
He doesn't do the pubs these days
Not since the cancer
When the radiothingy and the hormone crap
Was done
As if the music had been scoured out of him

Beach-walks with the dog now
In all weathers –
The sea is a grim business
Suicides and sea-wrack, but it suits him
The hills over the bay
Curved like a young girl's arse

Before the advent of that ache
Days were one come-all-ye
With victorie and with melodye
And in good compagnie
No tortuous walks in a face-splitting wind
To the dog-yap chorus of his ranting mind

A lewd imp in his ear
Where verses used to live –
No more of that, sweat and cigarettes
A late taxi purring like a panther
A guitar in its black case tugging at his arm
A girl's whisper: *I would, but I'm married*

Under the arc
Of the linear accelerator
In its click and hum he'd heard
Time's child's play calling time
And the lock on the pub's door going cluck
And he'd hung himself up with his coat

O for the days of gold, man
Raising the roof in The Tankery Inn
In a string-break
You'd ladle women into you
Tuning up, you'd tune them up
All music, all of it, a singsong tide of tepid beer.

Fred Johnston

ALL CLEAR

Life is all fleeting moments
but this one would resonate
through all choices thereafter.

She felt like a candle
being lit by lightning
when the good news came.

Told she was clear,
nothing sinister hidden,
no best-before date
to be stamped on any plans,
her smile shone, to spend
like a new-minted coin.

She was always the wrong side
of a door no longer there,
life running away
from her assumed fear.

Now she will move on,
have her hair done,
have her nails painted
a brilliant red, the proof
of being wildly alive.

She's going to star
in her own parade,
and tell the world
she will never be reduced
to anything less.

Gordon Scapens

Finally, the panic dies down and sleeps. But there is no comfort in that, because I know what's next. I start to feel heavy and numb. A shell forms around me. In defence of this I work, study, watch films, apply for benefits, talk to friends, get drunk, all the things you're supposed to do – I expect at least one of these to work, I have to, these are the only options I have, but nothing breaks through the shell. Things are looking black, and this is just the start.

When the chemist gives me the magic pills, I grab them, leave the shop and climb straight into my car and drive out of town. I head out into the sticks, further and further and park on the edge of a random dirt road. I jump out, leaving the engine on, and move quickly. I head down the road, step over a fence and walk across field after field after field. I go for hours. As the sky turns black and starry, I find a cabin, surrounded by trees and brambles and large green objects the size of buildings. Ahead there is the sound of a river. Tranquil, quiet, washing, but I see no stream.

I put my fist through the window. Glass shatters, blood runs down my hand.

Inside the cabin it's wooden, cosy. A stove and a table and a single chair to match the table. There is no WIFI, no phone signal here at all. My phone is a notepad, a calculator, nothing more, until it dies.

I sit at the table and put my head on my arm and close my eyes. With my free hand I pull out the box they gave me and slap it on the table. Only one thing is needed now – a thimble full of water every twenty-four hours, to wash one magic pill down a day. Supposedly they will start to work in two weeks and a human being can survive for up to eight without food, so food is moot. I only hope that it rains every night.

Thankfully, I find that the grass and trees around me are moist today, so the first hit is covered. Once I've washed it down, I pace up and down the cabin expectantly. My chest tightens, jaw tingles. A feeling between reality and ecstasy, somehow both and neither. After seven days, I'm feeling numb and bored. I have to keep reminding myself that the panic I'm staving off is worse than death.

It rains every night, and so every day I have no trouble collecting water from the leaves and washing another jigsaw piece of my new brain chemistry down and then starving all day and watching time pass.

On the seventh day, maybe the eighth, I start to feel dizzy. This isn't going quickly enough. In the second week I start double dosing, and then triple dosing. My head is swaying, the visuals strange. I lie on the floor of the cabin. Even here I can hear the river noise. What is it? What is this place?

Wake. Outside. Rain. Collect. Pill. Drink. Repeat. Sleep. Out. Collect. Drink. Pill.

After three weeks I don't bother going outside anymore. I just stick the pills on my tongue and swallow them and hope my body ingests them. I can feel them tapering down my throat, dissolving before they can be digested.

My throat is so dry. The emptiness unbearable. My eyes are like sandpaper, and I blink seldom. After staring up without seeing for so long, the cabin disappears around me. The wooden walls, the broken window, the roof beams – all of it. Outside, the trees are rustling, branches swaying and creaking. Beyond them, the rustling that could be water, but no... the more I listen the less it sounds like a river. It sounds more like...more like a metallic tangling. Chains clinking against chains. And something stirs in me. The first time I've felt stirrings in the longest time that I can remember. I'd be a fool to let this go.

Up. Out. Through the field, the trees.

For the first time I realise that this place is mine. It belongs to me. I never left town at all. I was always here. Beneath green growths there is concrete. Buildings, pubs, shops, houses. They're just covered in grass and soil now. Over there by the hill, amongst that complexion of large, square and rectangular green shapes, is where I used to work. And beyond a cluster of trees is one of the places I used to drink and try to grow up. And a hundred metres or so behind that, is a green slope that used to be a road. We got high there back in the day, when none of us had a home to go to, and sometimes we'd meet new people and behave objectively to get on. A memory for every step here. It's all here, just covered in grass and soil and flowers failing to grow.

In the only area not covered in growth, I find the source of the noise beyond the water. I'm an idiot for not realising this sooner. Between a rusty, rickety framing, a single swing sways gently in the breeze. The seat is withered and covered in bird shit and the chains are horribly rusted. This thing, I can't believe it's still here. I used to play on this as a child. I sit down and hold the chains. They feel rough and weak. I traipse my feet in the worn ground, rocking from toe to heal, creating a soft but undeniable motion. It's been so long since I've done this that I feel motion sickness even from that, and an instinct inside of me, one that I certainly created, implores me to stop. To slow down and get off. *Too old,* it says, *the swing is too old and you are too old for the swing. Get off, walk away.* But I do not. The motion gets pleasant and I swing harder, and before long I'm swinging so high that the frame jerks with every kick of the legs and the chains come loose as I reach the peak of height and then tighten abruptly on the way down. *Don't swing that high, you'll break your neck.* I close my sore eyes and refuse to listen. That voice was used on me when I was a child but now it's a part of me. I close my eyes and listen to the world and behind me I hear the chain snap, and I'm flung into the air, and the feeling as I surge through it is exhilarating. I see further than I've seen in years. I see where I went wrong.

This is only the start. Green is only the beginning. I own this place, and one day the trees will have transformed into netted cages held together by metal poles covered in soft foam and PVC, and the dirt and grass will turn into ball pits.

Max Watt

No family grieves my passing, no funeral is held,
No need to swill a sidewalk of the crimson blood just spilled.
Innocently passing, I froze in the flashing blue –
A victim of the crossfire, I fell and writhed on cue.
With bullets wildly spraying, I lie with eyes tight shut –
Scripted mayhem playing 'til the Director calls the cut.
I scramble back to life again, no call for grief or sorrow.
I collect my extra dollars and I'm back again tomorrow

Within this cavernous warehouse are fires of fury lit
But out there in the cinema seats is where the victims sit.
Assaulted by the images of each horrific scene,
Perceptions of reality warped on the silver screen.
Acclimatised to violence as each new film releases,
Inured to shooting, stabbing, torture – empathy shot to pieces.
In turn these victims victimise and easy vent their wrath
As normal as in film portrayed, their consciences switched off.

But on the real-world pavements, as gathered friends still grieve
Or silent at the chapel as parents turn to leave,
They mourn the death of decency, of empathy, of humanity –
Sponsored and promoted by cinema's profanity.
But no Director calls the cut, no crew restores the set
For in this spoiled reality – what you see is what you get.

John Fewings

Death plays a familiar trick
and comes through the front door like a friend.
He goes about his business in broad daylight –
right now he's in the next room smashing china.

He enters my bedroom before dawn,
folds his boiler suit over a chair
and begins reading tomorrow's paper –
I watch the smoke of his cigarettes.

With the final one extinguished
he looks up; the sun has risen and
we're facing each other like player and dealer –
I check my hand and lay down the King of Hearts.

He gets up and brushes away the ash –
look, he's coming over to settle accounts!
I'll part with the mortal share
and leave him to close the back door.

Iain Blair-Brown

GRIEF

wakes you every morning
faithful as a knocker-up
who tap, tap, taps
on your window.

Jean Stevens

His hair was almost stroked
by her trembling fingertips
on their brief second date,
but she withdrew her offer
when he pushed his head
into the palm of her hand.

He called for her five times,
with and without underwear,
as chirpy as testosterone
while he predicted her fall.

She stood behind the door
with the chain in her hand,
confused by his adrenaline.

Once he heard her weeping.
Once she repeated his name.

No question he killed her.

His single cryptogram of hair,
pasted with brown blood,
was found on her thigh.

Love is beyond forensics,
he repeated to detectives
and dismissed his lawyer.

His love was always a test
of her limitless forgiveness.

Only her body told the truth.

Robin Lindsay Wilson

The gun at the crime scene
had been fired six times.
There was only one entry wound,
so they brow-beat the killer
until he confessed to first degree
and five other things he hated.

Robin Lindsay Wilson

one road in
no way out
no up or
downtown
unsafe on
middle ground
dad dumbs down
mam comes round
wearing her
pound shop frown
kids sleep
unsoundly
dreams crushed
under the retail park
that sold out
when the unfair
came to town
nowt there now
unsend the clowns

Simon Tindale

Unscrewing a Marmite jar, I remark my phone ding. I check the notification as though the act is part of my reflex arc, and am disappointed to discover it's about someone posting a TikTok, an app I install and delete as one stands and sits, reaches out and in, goes from one room to the next. I can't get into it, don't know why I'm aiming to, either – just like how I have started drinking beer. I look at numerous shares of Instagram stories that I know are all important but pay attention to about one in ten, maybe even twenty. Twenty pounds was the amount in my wallet I was considering giving to a beggar four months ago, but I ended up lying that I had nothing, continued with my Christmas shopping. I've never believed in Christ, but for Christ's sake the Tories need to sort this out, rather than wasting two billion on a fucking boat for a dead guy. Then again, I walk as far away as possible from homeless people in the streets. The other week, I gave Azzie, the guy I told I had nothing, that twenty pounds I still had in my wallet towards a hotel. The other day, I finally gave a vendor three quid and a couple extra for a Big Issue that I'll likely never read, and I hope that neither of these people ask me for money again, because I'd struggle to say no now that I have said yes once. A different guy asked me for something towards a hotel the other night, too – I lied that time. I'll likely put this on Instagram, but if someone told me in person that they support the Conservatives, I would act rather conservatively, move on to a more light-hearted topic, like TikTok or toast toppings.

Terry Griffiths

It's the new way to do things apparently and I didn't want to be left behind
So took the leap forward and decided to order my life online
I didn't quite get what I asked for, however hard I tried:
Certain items were out of stock, so alternatives supplied.
I ordered a sense of humour, but got cynical disdain instead.
I clicked on a hint of roguish charm, coupled with a sunny disposition
But opened the box to find a sense of doubt,
Despair, and deep lingering suspicion.

I ordered a wardrobe of stylish tailored shirts and handmade suits
So what am I supposed to do with a dayglow thong
and a pair of deep-sea diver's boots?
They sent me an 8 Track tape of Orville the Duck
singing the hits of Sondheim and Lloyd Webber,
When what I ordered was a pair of snakeskin cowboy boots
trimmed in calfskin leather.
I then decided to order a player so I could listen to Orville's dulcet tones
But they sent me an arc welder, a rubber ring,
and two slightly camp garden gnomes.

I eagerly selected a giggling five-foot seven blonde,
complete with pneumatic wobbly chest
Instead, I got Graham the acne covered gamer
who hasn't been out of his room since the launch of Super Mario Quest.
It's gone beyond a joke 'Your item's out of stock so we thought we'd
send you this.'
Well it's just not good enough, they're starting to take the p*ss.
Same as it ever was, my life's always been a mish-mash
car crash collection of emotions and random things,
I want this nightmare to end ...
I've just placed an order for a loaded shotgun in sheer desperation,
now let's see what the bastards send ...

Neil Windsor

You look unsettled. I mean you no harm.
It's not compulsory, but a record would be kept
just to show that you had opted out.
You know what these things are like – once they're
there.

As I say, this is quality control.
So many third parties, so much information.
But we all share. We live in a community, don't we.
Yes, we all get on with our little lives.

You like your cup of tea in the morning,
toast on Sundays, you're a man of habit.
In bed, with the radio on, the classical music
– so soothing after such a busy week.

Phone calls, websites, where you park, how long
– you nip in for free half hours, don't you?
I don't blame you. All adds up, doesn't it?
No revenue if we all did that, though; eh?

We don't know much about your shopping.
You're more than skin and bone, so you must eat.
No loyalty cards. You use cash, do you?
But you use your card on the train, I see.

Your trips to London, galleries. You seem to walk
long distances between stations.
Fitness data we can only infer, no apps.
Ten K last year. Well done – such a hot day.

You're starting to see how it all works.
You saw a film three weeks ago. Was it good?
You bought two tickets, went with someone
not your wife, though. Is all well between you?

Of course. We have your well-being at heart.
And maybe times are not as happy as they were
– you at the cinema, a third party,
bluetooth vibrator busy at home.

Perhaps you think I've gone too far.
Time was, you might have spoken to a priest.
You think it's changed – it's all remained the same.
God has no monopoly on omniscience.

Stuart Handysides

REVIEWS

We are always happy to receive copies of newly published poetry pamphlets/collections, books about poetry, and poetry-art books which you would to have reviewed. These are offered to our team of reviewers who select what they want to review; generally speaking, about half the received books can be reviewed in any one issue. We discourage people reviewing the work of poets they know personally, as we feel it puts at a disadvantage poets who don't have connections to reviewers; if you have a friend who's published recently, get them to send me a copy and we'll add it to the pile. You may also submit a review you have written – no more than 300 words, please, and try to be objective about the book rather than just telling us you like it!

We aim to publish a balance between reviewing prize winning established poets (such as the very wonderful Forward Prize-winning Kim Moore whose two most recent books were reviewed in DC 45) and new voices, including young and emerging poets. We are keen to offer a platform to as diverse a range of poets as possible, showcasing all genders, ethnicities, neuro-diversities, and so on. Send books to the same address as all your written submissions: The Editor, Dream Catcher, 109 Wensley Drive, Leeds LS7 2LU.

Magdalena by Antony Christie
Maytree Press
ISBN 9 781913 508265, pp 32 £7.00

Christie's latest pamphlet is a journey into myth and legend, ranging from the apocryphal Gospel of Philip's version of the life of Mary Madgalene, to a fourteen century necromancer, peddling dubious relics. In this slim volume, he obliquely maps the ministry of Jesus Christ, from betrayal in the Garden of Gethsemane to resurrection, through little-read stories of what happened to his female disciple Mary Magdalene, who finds:

> 'a safe margin from which
> I stepped willingly
> onto the bank page.'
> ("In the beginning").

I've long had a soft spot for Mary Magdalene, who pops up in various guises in the canonical gospels, given their tendency to conflate a number of Maries within the stories. In a patriarchal narrative she stands out as the female other, often with the ability to see what is *really* going on. Christie uses her a spokeswoman for and interlocutor with for other largely unseen and unheard women, such as the young women utilised by Ghandi to test his continence in the eponymous "Brahmachari" (from the section entitled 'Delhi, 1948'). The appropriation of female experience is highlighted in "The Visiting Levite":

'... he was the first of many
Who have named me Eve,' we are told.

These poems talk about deeds, thoughts and intentionality, drawing on an ancient concept which I recognise as the 'logismoi', the thoughts which precede words and actions and which can be as spiritually damning as deeds themselves: Mary talks of:

'the bright stasis,
before thought, before knowledge;'
and 'I was his thought word
before it was tongue or breath.'
("Love Song").

Here is a collection about the human need to mythologise as a way of excusing the wrongs we visit on other people. It tells of the visceral love, grief and disgust of the subjects of such mythologizing, articulated by two women even less securely 'known' than the men whose deification defined their subordinate role. For the non-religious reader, there is plenty to intrigue, not least the neatness and energy of the language. And in the post-#MeToo/post-truth world, can any of us afford to ignore the voice of subjugated women? Dark, challenging, at times, yet overall, through these pages, we can hear the voice of Chaucer's Prioress, insisting 'Amor vincit omnia.'

Hannah Stone

Untanglement by Matt Nicholson
Yaffle
ISBN 978-1-913122-27-0 £10

The opening poem in this collection from Yaffle – once again an excellent book production – offers a view of the subject 'splayed like a bearskin rug' about to have what sounds like very unpleasant surgical interventions. If autobiographical, it suggests Nicholson is definitely entangled; fortunately, the remainder of the collection offers an opportunity to untangle himself.

That opening poem – "Said Big Me to Little Me" – closes with a promise from the former to the latter that,

'All I can tell you is, one day, when you're 48 years old,
another man, just as clever as the one inside your ribs,
will talk to you about all of this,
and I promise it will stop hurting.'

On the evidence of this entertaining collection, that promise was correct.
Nicholson seems to have taken the opportunity.

The early poems focus on childhood reminiscences and revel in the joy
of being 'Awake at sparrow fart' and on an excursion with mates –

'Well swing out in the unspoilt air
on the new rope over the beck.'
("Spontaneous forecast").

Nicholson certainly has the skills to draw the reader into the heart of the
poem whether it be listening to loud punk music in the bedroom next door
("1977(My Bedroom Next to the Revolution)") though

'Too young
to spell Anarchy
to appreciate
pretty vacancy.'

There is an edge to these childhood recollections and sometimes quite
gruesome taste and a random cruelty such as in an experiment in hole-
punching a butterfly's wing that the 'insect engineer' fails to repair by
silver foil and

'a teardrop
from the hot
glue
gun'
("Insect Engineer").

Always though it is the people involved who are the real focus of
Nicholson's interest – '…What's happened / to the lighthouse keepers?'
he asks on a lighthouse tour where he is bombarded by facts and figures
about the light ("Light at the End of the World"). A masterful poem – 'A
stoker rolled a cig' – is a delicate and awestruck paean to the hand-rolling
of a cigarette. Nicholson is clearly a close observer of those he
encounters in the normal run of life, those 'Strangers facilitating simple
transaction' ("Like hostages do") who become something larger in the
poems.

Some poems strain for effect – e.g. "Basic Transference" – but where
Nicholson's wordsmith skill and quirky sympathies work, they work very
well indeed. "Till the Day Breaks" is a poignant and powerful commentary
on someone unable to sleep where the emotional content is subtly implied
as, in the garden outside there is the 'whumping' – marvellously
onomatopoeic – of a barn owl's wing 'Just feet away from the fox so taken
/ with becoming a statue in the shrinking night.' In a matter of eight lines,

Nicholson has economically created an entire world. The collection is studded with arresting images – standing like 'unbailed stumps' ("A Cricket Field on a Yorkshire Wold"), a festival mosh-pit seen as 'a business of ferrets, writhing, / cast into this world on the spin cycle' ("Festival Ferrets").

Nicholson is a skilled poet who effortlessly draws out the emotional depths of the almost filmic vignettes of which he writes. In the pithy "Arrangements" the narrative takes second-place to the creation of an emotive mise-en-scène through images of displacement –

> 'I've no photographs
> of you except for one where
> you're standing by an open
> fire-escape'

and where the next meeting will be

> 'springtime
> in a cemetery, and the red
> ants will bite our ankles.'

He can also write tender poems underscored with wry humour – in "A Dream of a Day in a Gallery" the subject, not a lover of art it seems, is content for

> '…I'll be more than happy to queue,
> if I can spend a day as if I understand art,
> and I can spend that day with you.'

This untangling is well worth a read. Nicholson's writing pulls no punches but is delightfully featherweight rather than heavyweight. Maybe after all,

> '…winding the thread's
> the best bit by far.' ("Untangle").

Patrick Lodge

Ghosts Behind the Door by **Mig Holder and Tim Dowley**
Greville Press
ISBN 978-1-7399826-3-8

In this sequence of poems, siblings Mig Holder and Tim Dowley draw on memories of growing up in a sectarian family in post-war East End London. I grew up in a similar family. Though their upbringing was harsher, I recognise their portrayal of the fear adult religious zeal can cause a child, and the long-lasting effects of puritan guilt.

The collaboration works well with each author attributed by their initials. Tim Dowley is the main contributor. His poems tend to be short and hard hitting while his sister's often have a more reflective tone. Sometimes pairs of poems deal with the same subject from differing points of view, as in "Sealed" and "Passing it on (Sex Education)", or "Noli me tangere" and "His hands (the Chapel)". Both writers create vivid images. "Pianoforte" (TD) is only two stanzas long yet paints a memorable picture:

'Squatting beneath the keys,
I press the pedal with my fist,
probe under notes.

Behind the stool,
I smooth my fingers over the veneer.
Here they'll never find me.'

Mig Holder can also write with a similar telling compression, as in "Abandoned" – again I'm quoting the whole poem.

'It wasn't you they took me from,
they took me from myself.
They gave my heart to Jesus,
who left it on the shelf.'

1950s childhood is brought to life with telling details as in "Playtime" (TD) with its references to a wartime shelter, "Reckitt's Blue" and 'squeezing father's shirts through the wringer'. MH's response in "On Dolls Being Lowered from Bannisters" is equally vivid. There is a satisfying chronological development towards the death of the austere father whose loss his children cannot mourn, and the final poems are very moving.

I can recommend this collection, though with such dark themes it is not an easy read.

Pauline Kirk

The Ash of Time by **Penny Sharman**
Hedgehog Press
ISBN 978-1-913499938 pp 25 £7.99

Penny is a poet, photographer and artist and she is currently co-editor of *Obsessed With Pipework* Magazine.

The Ash of Time is Penny's fifth poetry publication and this latest collection promises to channel realism to explore her life and delivers with a series of verses exploring the emotional impacts of growing up and life experiences. In the first poem, "The Clearing," time is drawn back to reveal

'me the bairn
in all of this
mulch and canopy.'

"Lessons From the Larder Floor" is the only prose poem in the collection. It juxtaposes hiding in the larder (because of the relentless teasing the poet suffers from her brother) against her mother's acquiescence:

'she tells me she's always been good and let men control her life.'

The poet has other ideas after her mother warns her to run free:

'I Isadora my way to freedom one year after another.'

As might be expected of a collection published in 2022, there are obvious references to the pandemic, looking at rooms which constrain and yet allow the poet to dream. In "Pandemic Bedroom" the accoutrements of therapy are placed carefully on the windowsill:

'And when I close my eyes to dream
it's always you,
my soft skinned wizard that holds me steady.'

"Syzygy" is an interesting poem, setting up the conjunction of the full moon with the poet's mood swings and the dawn. It is also asking about the relationship of inside with outside using a paperweight as an example:

'the glass weight
a blue monster
phantom of the ocean
that says something is
connected in these words.'

The title poem of the collection draws several themes together, time with the poet's mum and looking to the future, finally asking:

'what's it all about
this life
this life'

The final line is left hanging without the finality of a full stop. There's a poetic chronology in this collection, room and relationships are explored with spare emotional language. I'll enjoy revisiting the Penny Sharman's poems in *The Ash of Time*.

Clint Wastling

the plumb line by Hélène Demetriades
The Hedgehog Poetry Press
ISBN 978-1-913499-33-4 pp75   £10.99

This is a debut collection from a prize-winning poet. The poems here focus very much on her childhood and family and pull no punches in their discussion of a complex father-daughter relationship and family life. There are elements of Sylvia Plath in this focus – daddy as 'ogre', monster, 'daddykins', the image of a bell jar-like 'cheese dome' fashioned by the ogre-father that is brought down on the family to stifle it. In 1981 the poet R S Gwyn wrote satirically of the younger poet who descends

'from Plath
and wanders down a self-destructive path
Laying the blame on Daddy.'

Demetriades cannot be placed within this category as, while Plath maybe chose resolution through her suicide, Demetriades works her way through the issues as befits a skilled and experienced counsellor and psychotherapist in courageous and compelling poetry that does not blame but seeks to resolve. She may plumb the depths in this collection but rises finally in some sort of accommodation; the bringing of the personal into the public realm with such bravery is both empowering and cathartic.

The book is structured in three sections with the first – "Beginning" – very much focusing on the child growing up in Switzerland, England and Boarding School – disorientations difficult enough without an unsupportive family context. When her accented English is not understood and she is asked if she is Cockney, she cannot tell – 'I lack the inner or outer geography to know' ("East Preston"). The relationship with her father the poems describe is caustic and corrosive – 'Daddy hits me   says I'm stupid' ("Ghost Mother"). As the poem's title suggest, her mother seems unable to provide what is needed in terms of love and succour. Throughout, Demetriades imagines a perfected childhood that is constantly undercut by her reality, expressed in discordant conjunctions – in "In My World" she imagines skipping to school '...in bright blue cardigan, April unbuttoned, the quilt of snow thrown off' only to see 'a rat corpse on the wall / I catch my breath at the heave-sea / flesh, maggots devouring it to bone tracery.'

Every silver lining has a cloud. She buys a stub of cactus and it flowers and spreads – on return from boarding school it is dead in the greenhouse – 'My father had taken against its unruly ways' ("Orchid Cactus").

The second section – "Gravity" – is dedicated to her husband and daughter and is life-affirming and full of images of fecundity and regrowth. The marvellous "Grace" has Demetriades, 'like a half-lit ghost' crawling into the skirts of a rhododendron bush where she too can blossom: 'The O of my ovum shudders dilates / It will swallow the earth.' She is re-wilded – the holly tree may wear its seeds on its crown 'mine are buried deep / but I flower just like her.' The final section – "Departure" – is dedicated to her mother and father and covers their deaths. The poems focusing on the death of her mother are sparse and elegant, though no less emotional for that. Those that cover her father's death hint at some sort of reconciliation, though that seems less an emotional and more a conscious and empowering decision. In "Daddykins" she offers to her dying father what she may have expected to have received from him as a child,

> 'I stroke your cheeks,
> whisper you sweet nothings,
> sing you broken bits of nursery rhyme'

but is aware that she is only trying to 'Conjure [him] into a loving daddy / with my breath.' The final line of the collection, where she gazes at the face of her dead father – 'I'm gazing at the mask of a Greek monster' ("Posthumous") – carries with it not the shock and horror of the first section "Daddy" but a stronger sense that Demetriades has moved on and, literally and emotionally, survived her father. This is an excellent first collection, harrowing at times but always lifted by the indomitable spirit of the poet and her gifts as a poet.

Patrick Lodge

On Poetry: Reading, Writing & Working with Poems by Jackie Wills
smith/doorstop
ISBN 978-1-914914-12-6 eBook
ISBN 978-1-914914-13-3

This is a big meaty book, impossible to do justice to in a short review.

Jackie Wills is an experienced poet and creative writing tutor. Her book is divided into two sections. The second, "Writing & Working with Poems" is full of advice on getting going as a poet, whether on your own or in a group, and gives practical hints for running creative writing groups. A lot was familiar to me as a tutor myself, but I appreciated the updates and fresh ideas. A newcomer would find this section invaluable.

I found Part One, "Reading Poems" very interesting. It introduced me to unfamiliar writers from the 80s and 90s, and the stress on women writers made me realise how much my own development has been affected by male poetry. There are essays on building a personal canon; deciding to write; Wills' own heroines and heroes; environment; setting and conditions, 'What gives me the right?' and politics and social engagement. The final essay on translation is a useful introduction to other cultures. Each essay is centred around an analysis of one or more poems Wills loves or has found liberating. She is particularly strong on Black women writers and lesser-known figures.

Wills sums up her intentions in her introduction: "The chapters in Part One are short essays that have come out of my reading. They explore how other writers feed what I write and that this is a continual process. I look at poets I read as a teenager and others I've come to later. I question the idea of a single canon through the lens of my own. I look at poets who keep me going because I admire what they're doing with language, metaphor or form, innovators and poets who answer back…. I hope these ideas will be springboards to further reading."

They certainly will be for me.

Pauline Kirk

The Bell Tower by Pamela Crowe
The Emma Press
ISBN 9 781912915996   pp 30   £7

I always enjoy engaging with the work of artists who practice in several different media, such as photography, music, painting, and given that Dream Catcher publishes freshly commissioned art work in each edition, I am perhaps predisposed to focus on poetry from such artists; they seem to convey a sense of someone able to communicate in multiple languages. Nick Allen's review of *Notes on Water* in this issue bears this out.

In the case of *The Bell Tower*, there is no art work included as such, although the production values of The Emma Press are undoubtedly aesthetically pleasing – thick, creamy paper, appealing cover design and a font which adapts well to frequent diversions into transverse layout, their format suggestion of the unexpected twists life can take. But we certainly have a rich smorgasbord of ideas to savour here.

Crowe's debut pamphlet – soon to be joined by another, while she searches for a publisher for a full-length collection – is sharp, playful, and deceptively clever. Here we see a poet provoking her neighbours over the issue of tree-felling (with a subplot of seduction); the eruption of each episode of '150 words as I wait for a Tree To Grow Back' (its sections subtitled anger, patience, courage, mercy) adding to a slightly surreal yet very grounded story. In other poems she identifies with Austen heroes, channels Marge Piercy and Fleur Adcock, eulogizies 'our dearest Wendy' in an affectionate 'Christmas Cope', and drops her last unused tampon into the only remaining cup of coffee in the house.

Crowe says of her practice that it 'focuses on words and how we say them, on text, voice and performance.' Having seen her read on several occasions, I can confirm the success of the last of those, and I think readers may be convinced of the high standard of other aspects of her work in this slim volume. There are plenty of questions and no easy answers; a yoking of the mischievous with the wistful. The ending of "All the Boys Go Soft and Sad":

'Is it how my three bowls line up
hot, cold, and halfway towards you, filled to disappointment
with no new normal?'

sends the reader down several different rabbit holes. I also want to commend a poet who has the courage to take on clouds, and find them more than fluffy and cute. If you are searching for catharsis in these bizarre and troubling times, I recommend "Cloudcunt," whose repeated, outraged 'fuck off' could speak for all us.

Hannah Stone

Impermanence by Colin Bancroft
Maytree Press
ISBN 978-1-913508098   pp 30 £7.00

Colin Bancroft has had many poems published and runs www.poetsdirectory.co.uk as well as 192 Press. His PhD is on the Ecopoetics of Robert Frost.

In his collection "Impermanence," we get the emotional impact of the temporary nature of life and love. The first poem "Tethered," juxtaposes a stormy night camping against the tragedy of his partner's miscarriage:

'That crush has come again
Though different now in the silence.'

Several poems examine the relationship of emotions and memories arising from the everyday events of life. The universal truth of impermanence is explored in "Marsden," through a description of the passing of a community which made its living from coal:

'All things that will ever come to pass
Will end up like these vague outlines parched in grass.'

The ending of the poem is a lyrical reminder of the pamphlet's theme. Looking through the collection I am struck by the shorter nature/single stanza form of many poems and also the rhythms and rhymes used by Colin. I have fond memories of being frightened watching the horror film, *The Fog*. Here Colin takes the narrative further. After buying fish and chips, the short cut across a misty playing field reminds the narrator of the film and he frightens his family as they sit at home. The drama of an average family is woven into several poems within the collection.

"The Broken Tower," reflects on the life of the poet Hart Crane. This is a heartfelt biography taking us to the heart of his suicide.

'He didn't write of the sailors
Passed out in drunken stupors.'

"After Frankenstein," imagines the doctor's wife taking up his experiments after being given her husband's heart. Too late does she realises of her creation:

'They were not him and could not fill
The monstrous chasm at my side.'

Nothing lasts and everything is in transition but these lovely poems invite the reader to explore universal truths through the ordinary. I recommend Colin's poetry pamphlet *Impermanence*. I'm sure you will enjoy it as much as I have.

Clint Wastling

The Rake Tristram by Fane Saunders
Smith|Doorstep
ISBN: 978-1-914914-21-8 pp24 £5

It is as well to start with the admission that while I am aware of Hogarth's sequence of paintings 'A Rake's Progress,' I'm not well versed in it, so any interplay between Fane Saunders' book and that older work of art has probably gone over my head.

There is a structure: 2 sets of 3 "Rake poems", followed by a "Laura poem" – Laura being his dead love – either side of a central "Unauthorised Biography Vol. IV 1730-1960", which takes 2 pages.

There are rhymes aplenty, assonance and wordplay – some of which is amusingly inventive:

'laura'd adore a
drop,'

'All-enveloping, our almost life

put the elope in envelope'

– as well as a tendency for words like "lugubrious" and "prestidigitation" which need some padding around them to avoid being a trip hazard for the reader.

"The Rake's Apology" is beguiling, with 'the apology' presented as a fox cub, wrapped in a blanket, and laid at Laura's feet.

'Do not worry.
Though it may break things, let it be your dog.'

The 'pampered fox became the dog' and reappears in "The Unauthorized Biography", a wholly satisfying poem which leads us through the decades of "The Rake's Progress", "Life with aplomb and sure-footedness – The Prison, then the Madhouse":

'myth.
And like all myths, not quite the thing it was,
elevated now to something less

than truth...'

'...his name dissolves: a sugar cube
relaxing into absinthe...'

The subsequent poem, "The Rake Packs up His Troubles" is an interesting play on form, with the opening seven lines of the sonnet being almost mirrored back through the final seven lines.

The closing poem "The Rake Makes Amends / a skipping song" gives the impression of the poet letting loose the reins and playing; there's an engaging almost nursery rhyme word association that bubbles and carries the themes of the pamphlet.

Nick Allen

The Storm in the Piano by **Christopher James**
Maytree Press
ISBN 9 781913508272 pp 35 £7.00

Christopher James' pamphlet follows collections with Arc and Templar and is an adventurous journey from Damascus to the banks of the Cam. Never before have I encountered so many funambulists, (and, yes, I had to look that one up), not to mention opera-going goldfish, and even Dorothy Wordsworth, sky-diving. Playful, provocative, this is poetry of a consistently high calibre: I was not surprised to learn that the majority of the poems had been placed in or won major competitions, including the National and Bridport, and that James was a holder of the Eric Gregory Award from the Society of Authors. Here is a poet ever exploring new places to people with imaginary and real characters. Sometimes these personnel perform whimsically: in "The Archbishops at the Lido," we find that:

'… Thomas Cranmer executes
a front crawl, as languid as a sinner to confession'

(though from what I know of him, Rowan Williams would be speaking Greek not Latin as he:

'gently chides a pair of pigeons
sipping at the shallows.')

Other characters provide the occasion for that poetic 'telling it slant': "The Liberation of Bayeux" sets a scene on 'D-Day plus one', when

'the sky stitches itself
to the sky, its rays woven through clouds'

in order to comment on the perennial theatre of war, from 1066 to 1945, the eponymous tapestry capturing images of other 'cartoonish soldiers' and 'ghosts of horses'.

A number of the poems are set in the turbulent arena of the Middle East. Here James shows an attention to detail which adds a deep humanity to the exoticism – "The Milliner of Hudaydah"

'trade[s] my hats for dates and pistachios,
coffee and raisons: the currency of hunger.'

And the members of "The Buddy Holly Fan Club of Damascus"

'traded vinyl for Molotov cocktails …Tarek sold his watch
for a passage to Greece and a tub of day-old falafels.'

The drama depicted in these dangerous situations is not denied, but never overplayed. Like the tightrope walkers he is obsessed with, James finds a breath-taking balance between the fantastic and the everyday. Strongly recommended, to bring light and noise into dull winter evenings.

Hannah Stone

Notes on Water by **Amanda Dalton**
Smith|Doorstop
ISBN: 978-1-914914-17-1 pp18, including photographs

Her sister has 'no idea how close I am to drowning.' This thin book on the devastation of grief, is told through, soaked through with reflections on water, its power, its ever-presence and the overwhelming power of flood. Because of this, Dalton's pamphlet sits well alongside Jill Penny's *In Your Absence*, Clare Shaw's *Flood* and Denise Riley's *Time Lived, Without Its Flow*.

Inventively or infuriatingly, depending how you feel about these things, the book starts at both ends – one end printed upside down, against the other. At their confluence sits a series of small black and white photographs. This device also allows the insistence of the idea flow, of unendingness; it is perhaps a Mobius Strip.

The stanzas come as sobs:

'in just seven weeks he goes
from coffee and wine
to peppermint tea
to tiny fruits
to water
on a spoon
to this –

just a drop on the tongue, like this
and when he opens his mouth for her fingertip
he's a fledgling.'

'She goes upstairs to sit with him

but it's easier to look at the photograph
– the one she'll decide to frame when he dies.'

How she makes an inventory of everything she remembers seeing on a walk, she had to take without him, as well as photographs:

'...and she saw how they didn't interest him, how they all looked
the same'

The work is immensely powerful – over-powering, perhaps – and brutal in the way it shows how a loved one can be ripped from our grasp with scarcely conceivable haste. The language of this devastation is spare, exact and beautifully crafted.

It is uncommon to read such a completely satisfying piece of work, although you may need to come up for air after doing so.

Nick Allen

The Illustrated Woman **by Helen Mort**
Chatto Poetry
ISBN 978-1-784-74322-2   pp84   £12.99

Helen Mort's third collection sees her going from strength to strength; already much celebrated and the recipient of prestigious awards, she was in the running for this year's Forward Prize for this latest publication. Am I the only reader old enough to have experienced a tingle of early memories of Ray Bradbury's short story collection *The Illustrated Man*, on looking at the cover of this 'essential reading' (John Glenday)? Mort has an equally compelling ability to tell stories, in this carefully crafted volume. (She is also an excellent novelist, and I do commend *Black Car Burning* for your attention.)

The Illustrated Woman features three sections, each taking us further beneath the decorated epidermis. "skin", the opening section, comments on the phenomenon of female tattooing, its taboos and delights. Here, as well as learning about Mort's own addiction to body art, we meet other 'illustrated women,' and are invited to reconsider the opprobrium cast on women who use this form of self-expression. "skinless" is altogether more personal in its focus, exploring Mort's experience of motherhood, which she presents as a visceral, utterly absorbing stage of life, which renders her into a new sort of animal. The intensity of the early months of childrearing, especially breastfeeding, returns her to an almost feral state of withdrawal from human society:

'At night, I turn into a mother grizzly,
my hands cudgels,
my voice dredged from my chest.'

Her son is the cub, whose first word is 'Teddy.' Mort conveys the simultaneously intense and isolated state of evolving into motherhood in a deftly understated way. "Into the Rucksack" describes the male mimicry of pregnancy intended to create empathy on the part of fathers-to-be:

'...into
the rucksack goes someone's earnest empathy, goes the guilt I
feel when I think about my own rucksack, how it is lighter
than some, into the rucksack goes my privilege, my
inexplicable pain. Now the men are patting their fake bellies.
Now they are taking the rucksack off again.'

The final section, "skinned", is the darkest part of the book, revealing the trauma of her exposure though the crime of Deepfake, about which Mort now campaigns. In this section, we again meet other women whose experiences Mort voices in sensitive and disturbingly honest words. An utterly satisfying read, and one that provokes so many questions you will return to it again and again, finding fresh answers each time to new questions.

Hannah Stone

Poetry for All
Sponsored by Make it York and Stairwell Books
BSL Interpreted by, Dave Wycherley and Vicci Ackroyd
National Centre for Early Music
25th November 2022

After a delay of over two years due to Covid, York Spoken Word held its third *Poetry for All*. Though originally scheduled for the Theatre Royal it had to be relocated due to the scheduling of the Christmas Pantomime.

Poetry for All developed as a response to an identified deficit in the world of poetry: a night with BSL interpretation and words on a screen for those who are Deaf or Hard of Hearing; a venue with everything on one floor for wheelchair users and others with mobility issues; and a place that is welcoming to those with sight loss: not too echoey, and with room for service dogs to sit by their owners. It was also important that wheelchair users and service dog owners could sit amongst their friends, and not be isolated in some set-apart ghetto.

The National Centre for Early Music proved to be the perfect venue. The acoustics are superb, for anyone depending on ears rather than than eyes; the performance space as well as access to the bar and other facilities are all on the ground floor; and the screen was large, at an excellent height, and thus perfect for projecting all the poems. This last part is important, even for Deaf audience members who can understand BSL: sometimes it's hard to see the interpreter if one sits too far away, and folk who are Hard of Hearing don't necessarily understand BSL, but can benefit from words projected onto a screen.

As Colly Metcalf observed in an email after the 2019 show,

> "Wow – it was absolutely worth it ... when's the next? I'd love to come again! Such a supportive atmosphere and people speaking words that I could understand.

> "For the first time I felt included in the poetry – by definition it's wordy and usually I have no clue what's going on... I loved that you had it interpreted and PowerPointed."

Once again, as ze has since 2018, the well-connected and brilliant Fay Roberts (ze/zir/they) was the co-host. Fay handles poetry bookings for the annual Edinburgh Free Fringe, and was our link to our 2018 headliner, Raymond Antrobus, who has gone on to win the Ted Hughes Prize. Fay brings a certain amount of magic. For maybe an hour after this year's event,

Fay patiently spoke or signed to all of the waiting YSJ students from the university's BSL course, who were delighted to meet a legend.

BSL interpreting is very physical and in previous years the interpreters were quite exhausted so this year the interpretation was shared between Dave Wycherley and Vicci Ackroyd.

Interpretation is not transliteral and in the case of poetry often involves the presentation of the idea over the words and it requires some preparation by the interpreter. An example is Dave Wycherley's interpretation of Tanya Parker's poem, "Shaping the Mystery", about watching a rehearsal of the Mystery (Waggon) Plays. There were gasps from the crowd, and later, much praise directed his way for how beautifully he interpreted the lines

'Marvels are made from sticks and sheets:
Canes change from canopy to pyre,
a blanket is both marriage bed and child.'

where a mimed blanket was folded up through and into his arms as an imagined babe. The result was magical.

The two headliners were perfect. Young Kizzy Wade, who has just started her first year as an undergraduate and is only 18, really "spoke" to the other students. Kizzy is a wheelchair user who performed poems about dressing as a Dalek for Halloween in a costume created by her and her school chums, and how humorous – and difficult – it can be to get around the very, *very* hilly city of Lincoln in an electric wheelchair:

'Finally, wheelchair accessible taxis absolutely cannot be Minis,
I do not need that kind of stress with a dwindling battery at the
top of a hill literally named 'Steep.''

Colly Metcalfe, who travelled down from Newcastle as a support poet in 2019, driving for ages just to do a single poem, had shown a real spark back then and had been selected as one of our 2020 headliners. She closed the show with poignant and gorgeous poems, followed by her own BSL interpretations of two songs, while the songs were sung and music was played. This brought the house down! The first piece was co-written by Colly. The image of a Deaf woman dancing and signing to this beautiful ballad will never leave me.

Our latest PfA actually did very well for a series that had been growing until Covid closures dimmed our trajectory, with 37 tickets sold, and 2 tickets comped, for a total of 49 attendees (including 10 hosts/poets/BSL 'terps). I am hopeful we can bring back this inclusive arts event next November/early December as part of York Disability Week, and ideally hold PfA 4, once again, in the wonderful NCEM.

Thank you to Make it York, York Disability Week for contributing toward the second BSL 'terp; Alan Gillott for recording and performing, Fay Roberts for hosting and publicising the event and to the volunteers who donated their time, bought snacks and drinks for all performers, and secured a second tripod to ensure at least one camera captured the event.

Rose Drew

INDEX OF AUTHORS

Other anthologies and collections available from Stairwell Books

For further information please contact rose@stairwellbooks.com

www.stairwellbooks.co.uk
@stairwellbooks

Lightning Source UK Ltd.
Milton Keynes UK
UKHW021827020223
416391UK00010B/72